IMPROVE YOUR IELTS

Writing Skills

Sam McCarter

Norman Whitby

فروشگاه کتاب مینیاتور
Miniature Book Shop
مرکز تهیه و توزیع کتابهای آموزش زبان
میدان انقلاب، روبروی سینما بهمن
بازارچه کتاب، پلاک ۷
Tel:66416858

D1208371

MACMILLAN

Macmillan Education
Between Towns Road, Oxford OX4 3PP
A division of Macmillan Publishers Limited
Companies and representatives throughout the world

ISBN 978-0-230-00944-8

Text © Sam McCarter & Norman Whitby 2007
Design & illustration © Macmillan Publishers Limited 2007

First published 2007

All rights reserved; no part of this publication may be reproduced,
stored in a retrieval system, transmitted in any form, or by any means,
electronic, mechanical, photocopying, recording, or otherwise,
without the prior written permission of the publishers.

Original design by Mike Cryer
Illustrated by eMC Design Ltd and Peters & Zabransky (UK) Ltd
Cover design by Andrew Oliver
Cover photograph by PunchStock

Authors' acknowledgements
The authors would like to thank Liz Hunt, Roger Townsend,
Micky Silver, and all the students who supplied the authentic sample
answers to the Practice Tests.

The publishers would like to thank Edward Leigh for his comments on
the sample answers to the Practice Tests.

The authors and publishers would like to thank the following for
permission to reproduce their photographic material:
Comstock p6(4); Image Source pp6(3), 70; Photolibrary.com pp(2), 42,
58(t), 62(b); Science Photo Library pp10(b), 62(t); Superstock pp6(1),
50(t), 58(b).

Although we have tried to trace and contact copyright holders before
publication, in some cases this has not been possible. If contacted
we will be pleased to rectify any errors or omissions at the earliest
opportunity.

Printed and bound in China

2011 2010 2009 2008
10 9 8 7 6 5 4 3 2

Contents

Introduction

What is *Improve your IELTS Writing Skills*?

Improve your IELTS Writing Skills is a complete preparation course for the Academic Writing paper of the International English Language Testing System. Through targeted practice, it develops skills and language to help you achieve a higher IELTS score in the Academic Writing paper.

How can I use this book?

You can use *Improve your IELTS Writing Skills* as a book for studying on your own or in a class.

If you are studying on your own, *Improve your IELTS Writing Skills* is designed to guide you step-by-step through the activities. This book is also completely self-contained: a clear and accessible key is provided so that you can easily check your answers as you work through the book. In addition, there is a sample answer to accompany each Task 1 and Task 2 question.

If you are studying as part of a class, your teacher will direct you on how to use each activity. Some activities can be treated as discussions, in which case they can be a useful opportunity to share ideas and techniques with other learners.

How is *Improve your IELTS Writing Skills* organized?

It consists of ten units based around topics which occur commonly in the real test. Each unit consists of three sections:

Task 1: exercises and examples to develop skills and language for Task 1 questions.

Task 2: exercises and examples to develop skills and language for Task 2 questions.

Practice test: a complete Academic Writing paper based on the unit topic to practise the skills learned.

Each Task 1 and Task 2 section is subdivided further into skills sections. These focus on specific areas of relevance to each task.

In addition, there are *Techniques* boxes throughout the book. These reinforce key points on how to approach Academic Writing tasks.

How will *Improve your IELTS Writing Skills* improve my score?

By developing skills

The skills sections form a detailed syllabus of essential IELTS writing skills. For example, key elements of Task 1 preparation, such as *Describing trends* and *Comparing information*, are fully covered. Similarly, Task 2 skills, such as *Expressing solutions* and *Developing ideas* are dealt with in detail.

By developing language

Each unit also contains a resource of useful phrases and vocabulary to use in each writing task. Over the course of *Improve your IELTS Writing Skills*, you will encounter a wide range of ideas to ensure that you are not lost for words when you get to the real test. These include concepts such as organizing words, trigger words, and linking phrases, which all contribute to an appropriate academic writing style.

By developing test technique

The *Technique* boxes contain short tips which can easily be memorized and used as reminders in the real test. These include quick and easy advice about planning, understanding questions, and how to use effectively the language you have learned.

How is the IELTS Academic Writing paper organized?

The academic writing component of the IELTS lasts one hour. In the test, there are two tasks of different lengths, both of which you must answer.

What does each task consist of?

In Task 1, you will have to write at least 150 words to describe some data or a diagram. Data will normally be presented in the form of a graph, a bar or pie chart, a table, or a combination of these. A diagram will normally relate to a process, the workings of an object, or changes in maps over time. You are always expected to summarize the information by describing the main features, making comparisons where relevant.

In Task 2, you will have to write at least 250 words on a topic. You will be presented with an opinion, an argument, or a problem, and you will be expected to respond in some way. For example, in your response, you may be asked to:

- express an opinion.
- give views about two different opinions and give your own opinion.
- discuss advantages and disadvantages.
- give a solution to a problem by suggesting measures.
- discuss causes of a problem and suggest solutions.

You are always expected to give reasons and include any relevant examples from your own knowledge and experience.

How will I be assessed?

In both tasks you will be assessed on your ability to express yourself clearly and accurately in English.

In Task 1, your answer is assessed according to your ability to write about data in an organized way and compare information where it is relevant to do so. You should write about the main features of the data and add relevant detail where necessary.

In Task 2, your answer is assessed according to your ability to write in a logical manner as you give a solution to a problem, present and justify an opinion, compare and contrast evidence and opinions, or evaluate and challenge ideas or arguments.

How much time should I spend on each task?

You are advised to spend 20 minutes on Task 1.

You are advised to spend 40 minutes on Task 2.

Even though Task 2 carries more marks, you should always do Task 1 first. This is because it is shorter, and psychologically it feels better if you have completed one task.

Change and consequences

Unit aims

Task 1

Describing trends
Related verbs and nouns
Understanding data

Task 2

Understanding questions
Expressing solutions
Linking phrases
Using trigger words

Task 1 Describing trends

1 The graphs relate to sales of media technology. Which graph a–h do you think shows sales for each item in the photos 1–4?

2 Match each graph (a–h) with the most appropriate description below (1–10).

1 Sales of audio cassettes fell steadily. ......*g*......

2 iPod sales rose gradually. ....

3 Plasma TV sales fluctuated wildly, but the trend was upward. ....

4 Sales of video cassettes fluctuated wildly, and the trend was downward. ....

5 Total digital camera sales dropped slightly.

....

6 Sales of audio cassettes fell and then levelled off.

....

7 The sales of MP3-players rose gradually and then climbed sharply. ....

8 Purchases of video cassette recorders declined dramatically. ....

9 Sales of games consoles decreased and then levelled off. ....

10 CD sales dropped suddenly. ....

3 Underline the verbs in 2 used to describe trends.

Example

1 Sales of audio cassettes <u>fell</u> steadily.

4 The verbs in 2 are modified by adverbs such as *steadily*. Find the adverbs and decide whether they mean slow or fast changes. Complete the lists below.

Slow ......*steadily*......,

Fast ....

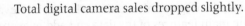

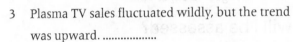

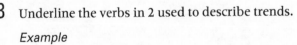

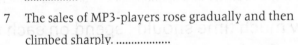

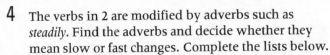

Related verbs and nouns

5 Sentences containing verb phrases such as *fell steadily* can often be rewritten using the correct form of *there is/are* and a related noun. Read the examples. Then rewrite sentences a–j below.

Examples

The consumption of chocolate *fell steadily*. (verb + adverb)
There was *a steady fall* in the consumption of chocolate. (*there was a* + adjective + noun)

There has been *a dramatic rise* in the production of films. (*there has been a* + adjective + noun)
The production of films *has risen dramatically*. (verb + adverb)

a   Spice exports from Africa fluctuated wildly over the period.

    There were ....

b   The development of new products fell gradually.

    There was ....

c   There has been a noticeable decrease in research investment.

    Research ....

d   The purchases of tickets dropped significantly last month.

    There was ....

e   On the Internet, the number of sites rose significantly.

    There was ....

f   There was a sudden decrease in the sale of mangos.

    The sale ....

g   At the theme park, there were very slight fluctuations in the number of visitors.

    The number ....

h   There was a gradual decline in sugar imports.

    Sugar ....

i   The quality of food in supermarkets has increased slowly.

    There has ....

j   The number of air travellers fluctuated remarkably.

    There ....

Technique

Include a variety of structures in your writing. Use both verb + adverb and adjective + noun structures in your Task 1 answer. Express nouns as *the ... of* or as two nouns.

6 Phrases such as *the consumption of chocolate* can often be rewritten as just two nouns. Read the examples. Then find and rewrite other examples in 5.

Examples

The consumption of chocolate can become *Chocolate consumption*.
The production of films can become *Film production*. (not *Films production*).

Understanding data

7 Read the graph and the Task 1 question. What was the income in dollars for:

a The Tea Room in January? ....$160,000........

b Internet Express in July? ....

c Wi-fi Cafe in November? ....

d Cafe Cool in December? ....

e The Tea Room in February? ....

Task 1

You should spend about 20 minutes on this task.

The graph shows the income of four cafes in New York over last year.

Summarize the information by selecting and reporting the main features, and make comparisons where relevant.

Write at least 150 words.

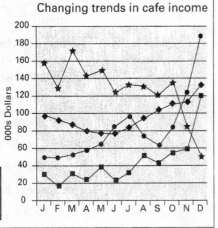

Changing trends in cafe income

000s Dollars

Legend:
- ★ The Tea Room
- ◆ Internet Express
- ● Wi-fi Cafe
- ■ Cafe Cool

Technique

To help you read the graph, write the names of the cafes at the end of each line.

---

8 Answer these questions about the graph.

a What do the letters J, F, M, etc along the bottom of the graph mean?

b What does 000s mean?

c What patterns can you see?

d What comparisons can you make?

9 Read the model text and decide whether each missing phrase is a verb, a noun, or an adverb.

Example

1 *adverb*

Model text

The graph provides information about the income trends of four cafes over the last year.

There are two basic general trends: downward and upward. As regards the first, the earnings for The Tea Room, were down over the year, falling ¹ .... from almost $160,000 earnings a month to just under $50,000 in December.

By contrast, the income for the other three cafes went up by varying degrees. There was ² .... in Cafe Cool's sales over the first ten months, followed by a sudden increase to $120,000. Furthermore, the income for both Internet Express and the Wi-fi Cafe ³ .... in December. The former experienced ⁴ .... to June, but after that, income rose ⁵ .... ending the year at approximately $130,000. Likewise, the trend for Wi-fi was upward. Between January to July, earnings ⁶ .... from $50,000 to nearly $100,000 and ⁷ .... to around $190,000.

It is noticeable that the income for The Tea Room is lower in the winter months than for the other three cafes.

10 Match options a–g with gaps 1–7 in the model text.

a steadily

b then rocketed

c doubled

d significantly

e also ended the year up

f a steady fall

g a rise

Task 2 Understanding questions

1 Task 2 questions contain a general subject and often include a specific **organizing word** to help you organize your essay. In each group a–d below, which **organizing word** has a different meaning from the other two?

a advantages drawbacks benefits

b measures steps reasons

c causes effects consequences

d disadvantages drawbacks solutions

2 Complete each Task 2 question below with **organizing words** from the box. You may use each item more than once.

agree or disagree advantages disadvantages causes solutions measures benefits

a What are the benefits of learning skills in the modern world?

b Any attempts to preserve the natural world will always hinder economic development. The benefits will however far outweigh the .... Do you .... ?

c What are the .... and .... of taking a year off between school and university?

d Students should be trained on how to cope with change in the modern world. How far do you .... ?

e Volunteer work with disadvantaged groups like underprivileged children is the best way for young people to learn about the real world. What are the .... of such work?

f Every day, animals are becoming extinct throughout the world. What do you think the .... of this are? What .... can you suggest?

g Overcrowding in large cities has always been a problem, but with populations around the world about to double, the social problems are certain to multiply. What .... can you suggest to control the problems?

3 How many parts are there in each question in 2? For example, (a) has one part. If there are two or three parts, how are they related?

Expressing solutions

4 Change is more rapid in the modern world than it was in the past. Number each category below 1–5 according to how rapidly each is changing in your opinion (1 = most rapid; 5 = least rapid). Think of an example of rapid change for each category.

Work   Technology   Travel   Communication   Health

5 Look at the Task 2 question below and answer the questions.

> **Task 2**
>
> *You should spend about 40 minutes on this task.*
>
> *Write about the following topic.*
>
> **More and more people claim that modern work patterns are a source of stress. What do you think are the causes of this? Can you suggest some possible solutions?**
>
> *Give reasons for your answer and include any relevant examples from your own knowledge or experience.*

a   Which part of the question states a problem?

b   Which two words in the question are important for the organization of your answer?

6 Read the conversation between two students discussing the problem of stress at work. Which part of the question in **5** are they answering? What solutions and results do they suggest?

Shen:	How do you think people can deal with their stressful lives, especially at work?
Tina:	Firstly, I think employers should encourage workers to relax.
Shen:	How?
Tina:	Well, in some companies, gym facilities or massage therapies are available.
Shen:	Massage?
Tina:	Yes. If you help your employees to relax, this improves their efficiency and production.
Shen:	Are there other solutions?
Tina:	Of course. Employees could be trained in how to plan their time more effectively. One way is to stop people taking work home. And then the workplace will become a lot happier.

Technique

Identify the type of question. For cause/ solution question types, include both and give reasons and examples. Organize your idea into an appropriate paragraph structure using linking words.

7 This paragraph suggests a solution to the Task 2 question in **5**. Complete each gap with the phrases in a–f for presenting solutions, examples, and results.

1 .... for employers to encourage workers to relax. 2 .... , in some companies, gym facilities or massage therapies are available. 3 .... , this improves their efficiency and production. 4 .... train employees in how to plan their time more effectively, 5 .... , by stopping people taking work home. 6 .... , the workplace will become a lot happier.

a   A further step is to

b   for example

c   I think the most obvious solution is

d   As a result

e   By doing this

f   For instance

8 There are several ways to express solutions. *Should* is used for strong suggestions; *could* is used for possible suggestions. Other phrases can also be used to express solutions. Read the examples from 6 and 7 on page 10. Then rewrite the sentences in a–f.

Examples

Employers should encourage workers to relax.
I think the most obvious solution is *for employers to encourage* workers to relax.
Employees *could be trained* in how to plan their time more effectively.
A further step is *to train employees* in how to plan their time more effectively.

a I think the most obvious solution is to encourage people to exercise more.

   People should ....

b The obvious answer is to reduce the number of working hours.

   The number of working hours ....

c The government could provide each employee with their own computer.

   One possibility is ....

d One option is to persuade parents to spend more time with their children.

   Parents could ....

e A good idea is to restrict the number of cars coming into cities.

   The number of cars coming into cities ....

f The government should build more skyscrapers to solve the problem.

   A good idea is ....

9 Which problems of modern life do the sentences in 8 refer to?

> overcrowding   traffic congestion   obesity
> lack of discipline   stress   technology

10 Use the following phrases to add results to the solutions above. Use your own ideas and words.

Example

a I think the most obvious solution is to encourage people to exercise more.
   By doing this, they would lose weight and would feel better generally.

> As a result,   This would enable/help them to   This would lead to
> This means that they would   By doing this,   Consequently,

Linking phrases

11 **Linking phrases** mark the **functions** of other sentences and phrases, such as solutions, results, and examples. Match each **linking phrase** with the correct **function**.

addition *and* purpose ....

condition .... reason ....

example .... result ....

and	consequently,
and so	since	for instance,
because	in order to
therefore,	if	furthermore,
as a result,	for example,

Using trigger words

12 Read the paragraph from a Task 2 essay on overcrowded cities and find the **linking phrases** which match these **functions**.

Reason   Result   Example   Solution

> Many cities in the world have now become very overcrowded because people are migrating in from the countryside in search of work. As a result, facilities like water supplies and public transport cannot cope with the demands from increased numbers of people, and so they are under severe strain. The obvious answer is to encourage the creation of jobs outside the cities. For example, we could encourage certain businesses to set up branches in rural areas.

13 **Linking phrases** can be used to trigger ideas because they mark **functions**. When you plan a Task 2 answer, write down some **trigger words** to help you develop your basic idea. Use the **trigger words** below to develop the ideas given.

A

If people migrate to cities, they become ....

And so ....
And as a result ....
A good idea would be to ....
By doing this, ...

B

People spend too much time watching TV.
For example, ...
Consequently, ...
If .... , then ....
This will lead to ....

C

The development of tourism often creates resentment among local people because ....
For example, ...
The obvious answer is to ....
Furthermore, ...

Practice Test 1

Task 1

You should spend about 20 minutes on this task.

The graph below shows in percentage terms the changing patterns of domestic access to modern technology in homes in the UK.

Summarize the information by selecting and reporting the main features, and make comparisons where relevant.

Write at least 150 words.

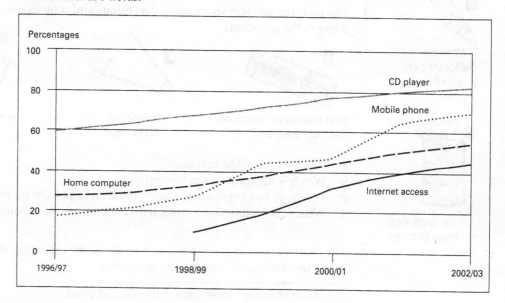

Task 2

You should spend about 40 minutes on this task.
Write about the following topic:

People naturally resist making changes in their lives.
What kind of problems can this cause? What solutions can you suggest?

Give reasons for your answer and include any relevant examples from your own knowledge or experience.
Write at least 250 words.

2

The importance of the past

Unit aims

Task 1	Task 2
Comparing information	Using *it/they/this/these*
Adverbs in comparisons	Planning essays
Comparing and contrasting	Developing ideas

Task 1 Comparing information

1 The pictures and text show some inventions and who invented them. Answer the questions.

Ballpoint pen, Laszlo Biro

Tin can patented by Peter Durand

First mercury thermometer, Gabriel Fahrenheit

Safety pin, Walter Hunt

Paper money in China

a Which is the oldest invention?
b Which is the most recent invention?
c Which do you think are the most and least important inventions?
d What other important historical inventions are not included here?

2 The chart shows the results of a survey about the most important inventions in the last 300 years. Answer the questions.

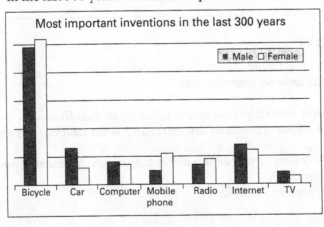

Most important inventions in the last 300 years

■ Male □ Female

Bicycle   Car   Computer   Mobile phone   Radio   Internet   TV

a What is the most striking feature of the chart?
b What voting patterns can you see for females?
c What voting patterns can you see for males?

Technique

In the test, circle and number important details in pencil.

3 You can use a range of structures to make comparisons. Read these examples describing the chart in 2. Then complete sentences a–j with suitable information based on the chart.

Examples

More males *than* females chose the TV. (*more* + noun + *than*)
Fewer females *than* males chose the TV. (*fewer* + noun + *than*)
The TV was *more popular* among males *than* females. (*more/less* + adjective + *than*)
The *most popular* form of communication was the Internet. (*the most/least* + adjective)

a   More females .... males chose the bicycle.

b   The bicycle was more .... than any other invention.

c   The car was .... popular among females than males.

d   .... invention among both sexes was the TV.

e   .... women than men voted for the mobile phone.

f   .... invention among both sexes was the bicycle.

g   .... males than females picked the radio.

h   The computer was .... for women than for men.

i   More people selected the bicycle .... any other invention.

j   The TV was .... popular than any other invention.

4   You can also compare information by using *as many ... as* when numbers are very close, or by using *not as many ... as*. Read the examples. Then compare male and female attitudes to cars and mobile phones.

Examples

as many females *as* males chose the computer.
Not as many males *as* females chose the radio.

5   Make comparative sentences based on notes a–g below and the chart in 2. Use the passive or active form of the verb in italics.

Examples

females/males/*select*/the bicycle	*More* females *than* males *selected* the bicycle.
males/females/*select*/the bicycle	*Fewer* males *than* females *selected* the bicycle.
the bicycle/*choose*/females/males	The bicycle *was chosen by more* females *than* males.

a   males/females/*choose*/the car

....

b   women/men/*select*/the mobile phone

....

c   the Internet/*choose*/males/females

....

d   females/males/*pick*/the radio

....

e   males/females/*pick*/the radio

....

f   the computer/*choose*/females/males

....

g   the bicycle/*select*/males/females

....

Adverbs in comparisons

6 You can add adverbs to comparisons to make them more precise, such as *significantly (more)* or *almost (as many)*. Read the examples. Then underline the adverbs in sentences a–i.

Examples

Significantly more people voted for the bicycle than the other inventions.
The bicycle was chosen by *almost as many* males *as* females.

a   Slightly more women than men voted for the bicycle.

b   In the past, considerably more people lived in the countryside than towns.

c   Many more people can use a computer today than thirty years ago.

d   Substantially less time is now spent doing housework than before.

e   There are significantly fewer people now working in manufacturing than in the past.

f   Sports programmes are watched by practically as many people now as in previous years.

g   The exhibition about cinema attracted far fewer visitors than expected.

h   Illiteracy is much less common than in previous generations.

i   Nearly as many children as adults watch programmes about ancient history.

7 Which adverbs above mean:
a   almost?   b   a lot?   c   just a few?

8 Look again at the sentences you wrote in 5 on page 15. Add suitable adverbs.

Comparing and contrasting

9 Answer these questions about the bar chart.

a   What do you think the bar chart provides information about?

b   What could the numbers on the left relate to?

c   What do you think the words along the bottom of the chart relate to?

d   What could the numbers in the box refer to?

e   Is there a time reference for the graph?

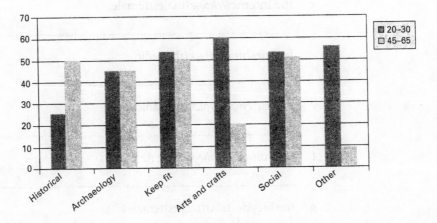

10 Match sentence beginnings 1–6 with endings a–f to form correct sentences about the chart.

1 The arts and crafts society has the greatest number of 20–30 year-olds,

2 Only 25 people from the younger age group are members of the historical society,

3 Some societies are clearly more popular with one of the age groups,

4 The keep fit and social clubs have slightly more members in the younger age bracket,

5 In general, the 20–30 year-olds are more actively involved in societies

6 The keep fit and social clubs attract a broader range of people

a *whereas* the archaeological society is equally popular with both.

b *in comparison with* the historical society.

c *but* it is one of the least popular clubs with the older age group.

d *compared with* the older age group.

e *while* the figure for 45–65 year-olds is about 50.

f *although* they are fairly popular with both age groups.

11 In which of the sentences in 10 could the ending a–f come first? Which connecting words in italics are followed by a noun phrase only?

12 Read the description of the chart in 9. For each of 1–6, two options are possible and one is incorrect. Delete the incorrect option.

Model text

Technique

In the test, make a quick list of the comparison structures you know before you write.

The chart provides information about how two age groups participate in several clubs at a centre for adults.

We can see from the data that the archaeological, keep fit, and social clubs are popular with both older and younger people. [1] *While/However/By contrast*, the historical and arts and crafts societies clearly appeal more to one of the age groups. In the historical society, 50 of the members are between 45 and 65, [2] *but/while/however* there are only 25 from the younger age group. For the arts and crafts society, the pattern is reversed.

There are about 60 members aged between 20 and 30, [3] *but/whereas/in comparison with* the number of people in the 45 to 65 age group is [4] *far/slightly/considerably* lower. The keep fit and social clubs are popular with both age groups, [5] *however/but/although* there are slightly fewer older people. Membership of the archaeological society stands at 45 for both groups.

In general, the younger age group are [6] *significantly/almost/noticeably* more involved in the various societies than the 45–65 year-olds.

Task 2 Using *it/they/this/these*

1 Read the text below written by a student as part of a Task 2 essay. Replace the words in italics with *it*, *they*, *this*, or *these*.

> Archaeologists, for example, help us to learn about the past. *Archaeologists* look for evidence in artefacts like pots and jewellery. *Pots and jewellery* reveal a lot of information about our ancestors. *Revealing information about the past* is very useful, but *the information* is still quite limited.

2 Match 1–4 with a–d to explain how to use *it*, *they*, *this*, and *these*.

1 *It* and *this* refer to
2 *They* and *these* refer to
3 *This* and *these* are often used to refer to
4 *This* can also refer to

a nouns at the end of the previous sentence.
b plural nouns.
c situations and processes.
d singular nouns.

3 Underline the exact text which *it*, *they*, *this*, and *these* refer to in sentences a–h. The first one has been done for you.

a History teaches <u>children</u> not just facts, but a range of skills. For example, *they* can learn how to analyse material, do basic sorting and research.
b Old buildings help create a more relaxing environment in cities than concrete office blocks. *This* makes them more pleasant to work and live in.
c Studying history may trigger an interest in other subject areas. *This*, in turn, may lead to other hobbies.
d Built-up areas can be made more attractive by adding monuments and statues. *These* can then enrich people's lives considerably.
e Governments should provide more money to preserve historical sites. By doing *this*, our heritage would be saved for future generations.
f Tradition does not hold us back as some people believe. In fact, *it* helps us to build the future.
g Schools and colleges need to emphasize history and related subjects as *these* will help give them a wider view of the world.
h The Internet and computers can be used to preserve the past. For example, *they* can be used by children to do basic research and store images.

4 Complete sentences a–g with *it*, *they*, *this*, or *these*.

a If the past is to be preserved, ... must be done by using modern technology.
b The art and language of a country represent its history, so it is important that .... are both preserved.
c The primary role of advertising is to encourage the public to replace the old with the new. .... is called progress by some people.
d History broadens the minds of most people who study ...., but .... also has the potential to narrow the minds of some.
e History should be given more emphasis in school, as .... will help children to understand better the world they live in.
f If history is emphasized more in schools, ... will lead to a better understanding of the world.
g The past informs us of the present and the future, but few people are sufficiently aware of ....

Planning essays

5   Read the historical facts in a–f below. Rank the events 1–6 according to how important you think they were in human history (1 = most important; 6 = least important). What other events would you add to the list?

a   In 1792, France abolished the monarchy and instituted the first republic.
b   In 1953, Francis Watson and James Crick described the structure and importance of DNA.
c   In October 1492, Christopher Columbus set foot in the Americas.
d   In 1885, Karl Benz built and patented the first automobile.
e   In 1983, a computer system connecting universities was created, which later became the Internet.
f   In the ninth century, gunpowder was first invented and used by the · Chinese.

6   Read the Task 2 essay question below. Decide which of points a–g are relevant to this answer.

> *It is sometimes said that history never repeats itself, yet there is much in it which is relevant to our modern world. Suggest some ways in which the study of history might help us today.*

a   There is often uncertainty about what really happened with regard to well-known historical events.
b   Studying other historical periods gives insights into different ways of life.
c   We can learn about the recent past by asking older relatives.
d   History involves investigation and interpretation, so its study develops thinking skills.
e   Learning about conflicts in the past can teach us how to avoid them in future.
f   History is a more difficult area of study than most people imagine.
g   The past can often provide explanations for the situations we face today.

7   Read the idea below. Choose some of the **trigger words** to develop this point. The first one has been done for you. Refer to Unit 1 page 12 for more examples of similar phrases.

Studying other historical periods gives insights into different ways of life.

For example, *students can investigate the way in which people lived in ancient times*

such as ....

As a result, ...

Therefore, ...

Furthermore, ...

8   Look back at the other relevant sentences you chose in 6 above. Develop those ideas in the same way using trigger words. Then write out your ideas in a paragraph.

Developing ideas

9 Read the Task 2 question below. Make a note of any ways you can think of to make history more interesting.

> *Some children find learning history at school very exciting, but many others think it is very boring. In what ways can history be brought to life for all school children?*

10 The list a–i below contains ideas that a student came up with for the essay question in 9. There are three solutions, each with an example and an effect. Complete the table by matching each idea with the appropriate **function**.

	Paragraph 1	Paragraph 2	Paragraph 3
Solutions	*a*		
Examples			
Effects			

    a   using the Internet and computers

    b   visiting historical sites

    c   historical places seem more real

    d   make a poster about local history

    e   go to a local archaeological site

    f   it increases motivation to do research

    g   these skills can be applied in other subjects

    h   doing written projects

    i   search for information about historical figures online

11 Decide which **function** in 10 these **linking phrases** relate to.

    a   Another method is to

    b   This will lead to

    c   For example,

    d   Last but not least, children could

    e   For instance,

    f   such as

    g   As a result,

    h   The best way is to

    i   Then

Technique

To help you build a bank of ideas, recycle relevant information from other essays.

12 Use your answers to 10 and 11 to write the ideas out as three paragraphs.

Practice Test 2

Task 1

You should spend about 20 minutes on this task.

The graph below shows the contribution of three sectors – agriculture, manufacturing, and business and financial services – to the UK economy in the twentieth century.

Summarize the information by selecting and reporting the main features, and make comparisons where relevant.

Write at least 150 words.

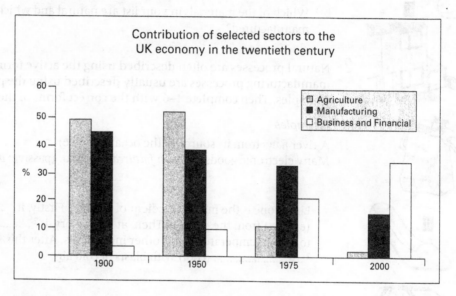

Task 2

You should spend about 40 minutes on this task.
Write about the following topic:

To some people studying the past has little value in the modern world. Why do you think it is important to do so? What will be the effect if children are not taught history?

Give reasons for your answer and include any relevant examples from your own knowledge or experience.
Write at least 250 words.

Machines, cycles, and processes

Unit aims

Task 1

The passive
Sequencing

Task 2

Using *which* to organize information
Expressing result and purpose

Task 1 The passive

1 Look at the five objects a–e and answer the questions.

a Which materials are used to make these objects?

b Which of the materials in your list are natural and which are manufactured?

2 Natural processes are often described using the active form, whereas manufacturing processes are usually described using the passive. Read the examples. Then complete 1–6 with the correct forms of the verbs in brackets.

Examples

A river *flows* from its source to the ocean. (active)
Many electronic goods *are manufactured* in Japan. (passive: *be* + past participle)

Limestone is the main ingredient of cement. Firstly, it [1] .... (extract) from the ground. Then, at the factory, it [2] .... (heat) to a high temperature with other ingredients. After this, it [3] .... (cool) with blasts of cold air.

When warm air [4] .... (reach) high ground, it is forced to rise, and, as a result, it [5] .... (cool). Moisture in the air [6] .... (condense) to form rain.

Technique

When describing processes, show that you can use active and passive forms where appropriate.

3 When describing processes, make sure the subject and verb agree. Read the example, then complete 1–8 with the correct forms of the verbs in brackets.

Example

The sun *shines* and the temperature *rises*.

Some rock formations [1] .... (hold) large amounts of water. When it [2] .... (rain), the tiny spaces in the rock gradually [3] .... (fill) with water so that the rock [4] .... (become) saturated. The top of this saturated zone is called the water table. If long periods of rain [5] .... (occur), the water table [6] .... (rise). If there is no rain, the rock [7] .... (begin) to dry out and the water table [8] .... (fall).

4 Verbs which require an object are called transitive. Verbs which never have an object are called intransitive. Are the verbs in sentence a–c transitive, intransitive, or both? Which sentence cannot be put into the passive?

a The temperature *falls*.
b Manufacturers *make* rubber products.
c Sunlight *opens* the leaves. The leaves *open*.

5 Put each verb in the box into the correct list: transitive, intransitive, or both.

~~fall~~	design	produce	rise	send	begin	manufacture
	obtain	die	become	dry	grow	cool

Transitive:
Intransitive: fall
Both:

6 Use the notes below to write short paragraphs about production processes.

Example

The production of a car involves various stages. car/design; prototype/make; car/mass-produce; car/distribute; car/sell
After the car is designed, a prototype is made and the car is mass-produced. The car is then distributed and sold.

a The production of a motorcycle involves various stages. motorcycle/design; prototype/make; prototype/test; motorcycle/manufacture; motorcycle/export; motorcycle/sell.
b The diagram shows the various stages in the production of bread. wheat/plant; crop/harvest; wheat/transport to the mill; wheat/make flour; flour/buy/baker; bread/bake; bread/sold.

7 Some diagrams require descriptions using past tenses. Complete the paragraph with the verbs from the box.

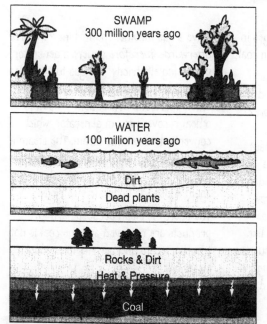

SWAMP
300 million years ago

WATER
100 million years ago

Dirt

Dead plants

Rocks & Dirt

Heat & Pressure

Coal

a died and dropped	b was formed
c lived	d was covered	e was trapped
f turned	g is now mined	h built up

The diagrams show the process by which coal
[1] .... over a period of millions of years.
First of all, large plants [2] .... in enormous swamps a long time ago. These [3] .... to the bottom of the water. Over the years, the dead plants formed a layer, which became deeper and deeper. More and more earth and dirt
[4] .... on top of this layer. Subsequently, this layer [5] .... by rocks and dirt, and so the energy of the dead plants [6] .... underneath. As the pressure and the heat grew over time, the layer of dead plants [7] .... into coal. Seams of coal were formed, and coal [8] ....

Sequencing

8 The diagram shows how energy is produced from coal. Answer the questions.

a How is the coal carried to the power plant?
b What is added to the furnace in addition to coal?
c What gas is produced when coal is burnt in the furnace?
d What do you think is removed from the gas?
e What is the gas called following this process?
f What do you think the gas does in the turbine?
g What does the turbine do to the generator?
h Where do the hot exhaust gases come from?
i What happens to the gases?

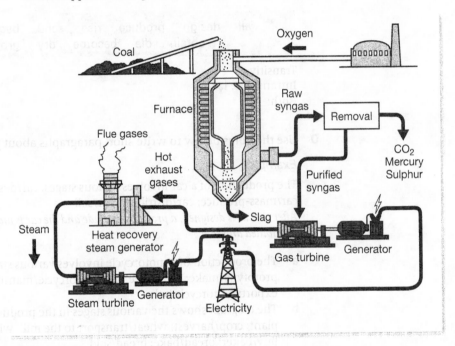

9 Complete the model text below by choosing the correct alternative in each case.

Model text

Technique

When describing processes, use phrases such as *First of all*, *After that*, and *When* as trigger words to help you sequence ideas.

The diagram shows the various stages in the production of clean energy from coal.

[1] *First of all/At first/One*, the coal is mined in deep pits underground and then carried to the surface. [2] *Furthermore/ After that/As a result*, it is carried along a conveyor belt to a power plant, [3] *when/then/where* it is burned in a large furnace to which oxygen is added. [4] *Otherwise/From this/Therefore*, raw syngas is produced. At the next stage of the process, harmful substances like carbon dioxide, mercury, and sulphur are removed. [5] *Following that/ Following/ Subsequent*, the purified gas is used to

drive a gas turbine. The turbine [6] *in turn/ afterwards/therefore* powers a generator, producing electricity. The gas turbine also produces hot exhaust gases. These are [7] *then/therefore/consequently* piped to a heat recovery steam generator, which converts the heat into steam. The steam is [8] *consequently/subsequent/subsequently* used to power a steam turbine, which again is used to generate electricity.

The energy is clean because harmful products are removed and the coal is not transported to another site to produce electricity.

10 Connect the sentences below. Use the **linking words** in brackets in each case.

Example

The parts of the car are assembled. The cars are exported. (after)
After the parts of the car are assembled, the cars are exported.

a   The snow falls. It covers the ground with a protective layer. (when)

....

b   Her cubs are born. The lioness licks them all over. (as soon as)

....

c   The paper is collected. It is sent for recycling. (once)

....

d   Volcanoes erupt. They send huge amounts of smoke into the air. (before)

....

e   The plants perspire. The air becomes humid. (when)

....

f   The trees are cut down. The forest is gradually destroyed. (and)

....

11 Connect these sentences using your own words.

a   The food is processed. It is packaged. It is distributed.

....

b   The cycle is completed. It repeats itself all over again.

....

c   The rubbish is collected. It is sent to a centre for sorting. It is recycled.

....

d   A new model of the bicycle is developed. The bicycle is tested.

....

e   The TV is assembled. It is sent to the shops.

....

f   The water is purified. It is bottled.

....

g   The data about the weather is collected. The information is then broadcast.

....

h   The prototype is tested. It is modified.

....

12 From your own knowledge, write a short paragraph to describe each of the processes below.

a   The process of digital photography from the action of taking a photograph to displaying the image.

b   The progress of a letter or parcel from packaging to delivery.

c   The life cycle of an animal such as a butterfly or a frog.

d   The water cycle which creates clouds and rainfall.

1 Answer the questions about the list of technologies.

> computers   automatic doors   mobile phones   video games
> TV remote controls   MP3-players   satellite navigation systems
> digital cameras

a Which of the technologies can help people and which can make life more difficult?

b Which technologies might make people more lazy?

c Which technologies do you find annoying and which impressive?

2 Read the Task 2 question. What two key elements must you include in your answer? Underline the **organizing words** which tell you this.

> *A recent survey has shown that people of all ages are losing the ability to perform basic practical tasks and processes at work. What do you think are the main causes of this? What solutions can you suggest?*

3 Read the following paragraph written by a student and answer questions a–e.

> People generally are losing traditional practical skills which they need to function in everyday life. This has come about, in my opinion, because people are now so over-reliant on machines. For example, computers in one form or another perform many of the tasks that people used to do themselves such as office functions, opening and locking doors, or switching machines on and off. Consequently, workers cannot do basic practical tasks in depth, which in turn has an impact on how to process basic information mentally when they are at work.

a What kind of skills are people losing?

b What is the cause of this?

c Which examples are given?

d What is the practical consequence of all this?

e What is the mental consequence?

4 In each sentence below, what does the word in italics refer to?

a People often allow the TV to do their thinking for them at home, *which* in turn has an impact on their mental performance at work. (Effect)

b People generally are losing traditional practical skills *which* they need to function in every day life.

5 Combine the following pairs of sentences using *which*.

a Sometimes, computers make mistakes and prevent things happening. This wastes valuable time and can cost money.

....

b TV programmes provide people with information about the world around them. This information is often very useful.

....

c Machines now give us more freedom. This means that we have more time for leisure activities.

....

d Technology saves us more and more time. This time can be used to create more machines.

....

e More and more household tasks are now carried out by robots. They will be even more common in the future.

....

f Everything seems to be available at the touch of a button. This makes people expect instant responses from other people.

....

Technique

Use *which* as a trigger word to add detail to your writing.

6 What does *which* refer to in each of your answers in 5? In which cases does the *which* clause express an effect as in 4a?

7 When combining sentences, a *which* clause often contains information that is non-essential to the sentence. Read the examples. Then combine the sentences in a–e, deciding which information is non-essential.

Examples

News broadcasts about world disasters, *which* are now available 24 hours a day, can make people feel anxious.

The situation, *which* people blame the government for, is everyone's fault.

a The situation has now become much more complex. It is effectively out of control.

....

b The problem is everyone's responsibility. The public blame the government for it.

....

c The cause of the problem is the lack of basic training. The cause is not immediately obvious to everyone.

....

d The solution is, in my opinion, by far the best. The solution is to have a day at work where people do not use computers or other machines.

....

e Office technology is the cause of much frustration at work. It requires only basic training to use.

....

Expressing result and purpose

8 The extract below contains three paragraphs, each organized to express **functions** such as cause and result. Identify the ideas that relate to each **function** and underline them. The first paragraph has been done for you.

Problem —

First of all, in recent years, many people all over the world have demonstrated <u>a clear lack of ability to carry out certain basic tasks</u>. A number of reasons have been put forward for this, but by far the most important, I feel, is <u>the complexity of the modern age</u>.

Cause —

Parents, for example, no longer have enough time to spend at home with their children, because many are working unsociable hours to cope with the pressures and demands of today's world. Young people are consequently deprived of valuable time to learn the practical skills necessary for everyday life like

fixing a plug, mending a puncture on a bicycle, or even sewing a button on a shirt.

Apart from parents, the international drive towards learning new technology also needs to carry a good part of the blame. This has led to young people leaving school literate in certain computer skills. But it has also created a generation almost deficient in basic practical skills, because technical problem-solving like making things in carpentry has been squeezed out of the school curriculum.

Paragraph 1: Problem/Cause

Paragraph 2: Example/Cause/Effect

Paragraph 3: Cause/Result 1/Result 2/Reason/Example

9 Which linking phrases are used in 8 to express the **functions** listed?

10 Decide whether the **linking phrases** below express Result or Purpose.

> so   therefore   in order to   consequently   so as to   as a result
> with the aim of   and so   so that   for this reason   as a consequence
> hence   which leads to   which means that

Technique

Learn at least one result phrase and one purpose phrase and use these as trigger words. When you write a sentence, insert your result/purpose trigger words to develop it.

11 For each idea below, continue the sentence or write a follow-on sentence using your own ideas to express Result or Purpose.

a   Children are now learning how to do mental arithmetic again.

....

b   Some cities charge motorists to take their cars into the centre.

....

c   Machines are manufactured to break down after a certain time.

....

Practice Test 3

Task 1

You should spend about 20 minutes on this task.

The diagram below shows how salt is removed from sea water to make it drinkable.

Summarize the information by selecting and reporting the main features, and make comparisons where relevant.

Write at least 150 words.

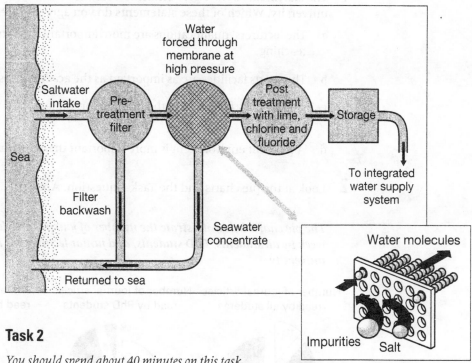

Task 2

You should spend about 40 minutes on this task.
Write about the following topic:

The widespread use of the Internet has brought many problems. What do you think are the main problems associated with the use of the web? What solutions can you suggest?

Give reasons for your answer and include any relevant examples from your own knowledge or experience.
Write at least 250 words.

4 *Education*

Unit aims

Task 1	Task 2
General and specific statements	Avoiding overgeneralization
Comparing information	Developing reasons
Describing proportions	

Task 1 General and specific statements

1 The statements below give students' reasons for choosing a particular university. Which of these statements do you agree with?

  a   The lecturers' qualifications are more important than the quality of the teaching.

  b   The sports facilities are as important as the academic resources.

  c   Good library facilities are the most important factor for postgraduate students.

  d   A pleasant environment is more important than the university's reputation.

2 Look at the pie charts and the Task 1 question. Answer questions a–e below.

The pie charts below illustrate the number of journal articles read per week by all students, PhD students, and junior lecturers at an Australian university.

Number of journal articles read by all students Number of journal articles read by PhD students Number of journal articles read by junior lecturers

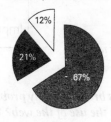

■ 1 to 5   ■ 6 to 11   □ 12+

Summarize the information by selecting and reporting the main features, and make comparisons where relevant.

  a   What does each pie chart describe?

  b   What do the numbers on each pie chart represent?

  c   What does the box at the bottom of the pie charts refer to?

  d   What noticeable feature can you see in each chart?

  e   What general statements can you make about each chart?

3 Complete sentences a–g using the phrases below.

> that   respectively   for example   how   but
> which   meanwhile   whereas   and

a   The three pie charts illustrate .... many articles from academic journals are read weekly by PhD students .... junior lecturers compared to other students at an Australian university.

b   .... the overwhelming majority of those studying doctorates read at least twelve articles per week in comparison with the average student.

c   The figures were 80 per cent and twelve per cent ....

d   Furthermore, only five per cent of PhD level students read between one and five articles, ... the average for all students in this category is a hefty 67 per cent.

e   .... , for junior lecturers the pattern appears to be slightly different.

f   Most read six or more articles per week (99 per cent), ... out of this total 24 per cent read twelve or more, ... is almost a third of the corresponding figure for PhD level students.

g   It is clear .... those students who are researching for a PhD read more articles than either junior lecturers or other students.

4 The sentences in 3 form a model text. Group the sentences into four paragraphs.

Paragraph 1:   ....
Paragraph 2:   ....
Paragraph 3:   ....
Paragraph 4:   ....

5 Descriptions contain general and specific statements. **Specific statements** contain reference to data, whereas **general statements** do not. Which statements in 3 are **general**? Which are **specific**?

6 Divide the following sentences into **general** and **specific statements**.

Examples

General: Postgraduate students tended to be better off than other students.
Specific: Seventy-five per cent of school children read comics each week.

a   Far fewer female lecturers as opposed to male lecturers are employed at the university, 25 and 75 respectively.

b   We can see that there are considerable differences in the proportion of nationalities in each course.

c   Only ten per cent of students preparing for their Masters attended taught classes.

d   Overall, women were more likely to read novels than men.

e   Students preparing for their doctorate read the greatest number of journal articles.

f   The sales for all four companies showed similar trends.

g   The pattern for senior lecturers was very different.

h   The vast majority of those students preparing for PhDs read twelve or more journal articles each week.

Technique

Aim to make at least one general statement in the middle of your text.

31

Comparing information

7 Rewrite the following sentences using the given words so that the meaning is the same.

a Far more PhD students read over twelve articles a week compared with junior lecturers.
Far fewer ....

b The average student reads fewer journal articles than the average junior lecturer.
The average junior lecturer ....

c The other students at the university do not read as many articles as the average PhD student.
The average PhD student ....

d Junior lecturers do not have as much time to read articles as those students who are researching for a PhD.
Those students who are researching for a PhD ....

Describing proportions

8 The phrases in the list are alternative ways of describing proportions. Divide the list into four groups that each have similar meanings.

> three quarters   almost half   one third   75 per cent   one in three
> nearly half   26 per cent   48 per cent   about one in four   33 per cent
> three out of four   just under one half   just over a quarter
> close to one half

9 These adjective-noun collocations can also be used to describe proportions. Write the adjectives next to the correct meaning in the table.

> the *vast* majority   a *tiny* minority   a *massive* 85 per cent
> a *modest* twelve per cent   a *hefty* 85 per cent
> a *mere* twelve per cent   the *overwhelming* majority

Very big	....
Very big (used before numbers)	....
Very small	....
Not very big (used before numbers)	....

Technique

Vary the way you express proportions – sometimes use words instead of numbers.

10 Rewrite sentences a–e, replacing the phrases in italics with an alternative expression.

a We see from the chart that *23 per cent* of students failed to finish their university degree.

b In 1990, *nine out of ten* engineering students were male, but by 2000 this figure had fallen to *exactly three quarters*.

c In 1960, *34 per cent* of science graduates went into the teaching profession but in 1970, the figure was just *ten per cent*.

d *Exactly one half* of the student population were members of the union in 2001, but five years later the figure was *64 per cent*.

e *Ninety-two per cent* of people surveyed felt that mixed sex schools were preferable.

11 Read the Task 1 question below and answer questions a–e.

Task 1
The pie charts below show the number of hours spent in a British university library by undergraduates, postgraduates, and the total student population.

Proportion of all students
by time spent in library

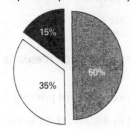

Proportion of undergraduates by
time spent in library

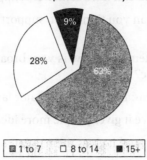

Proportion of postgraduates by
time spent in library

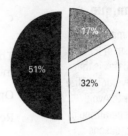

■ 1 to 7   □ 8 to 14   ■ 15+

Summarize the information by selecting and reporting the main features, and make comparisons where relevant.

a What are the similarities between postgraduate and all students?

b What are the main differences between undergraduate and postgraduate students?

c What tendency can you observe as students move from undergraduate to postgraduate?

d What is the most interesting feature of the three charts?

e What general conclusions can you draw?

12 Choose the most suitable alternative to complete the sentences below about the data in 11.

a Meanwhile, the *pattern/amount/majority* for postgraduate students was substantially different.

b Overall, the *pattern/size/proportion* of postgraduate students who spent fifteen hours a week or more in the library was very close to the entire student body who spent 1–7 hours in the library.

c The most striking difference in the data for undergraduates was that a sizeable *majority/minority/number* spent only 1–7 hours per week in the library.

d A *majority/minority/total* of undergraduates (nine per cent) used the library for fifteen or more hours per week.

e There is a clear *trend/progress/drift* towards using the library more as students move towards graduation and post-graduation.

f Undergraduate students were less likely than postgraduate students to use the library with just under *one quarter/one third/two-thirds* of the former spending 1–7 hours there.

g About a *third/quarter/minority* of undergraduate students as opposed to nearly a third of postgraduate students spent between eight and fourteen hours studying.

13 In your own words, write two sentences about each pie chart and one summarizing sentence.

1 Read the sentences below. Then answer questions a–c.

- The international community should ensure that education is free for all schoolchildren.
- They should provide books.
- Parents should be encouraged to become involved in schools.

a   How are the ideas connected?

b   Do the second and third sentences support the first sentence?

c   What ideas can you think of to support the first sentence?

Technique

A common criticism of IELTS candidates is that they overgeneralize in Task 2. Avoid overgeneralizing by giving reasons.

2 The opinion statement below is very broad. In your opinion, which reason is most appropriate?

Opinion statement: Education is a major factor in lifting people out of poverty

Reason 1: … since it gives people more ideas about what to do with their lives.

Reason 2: … because it gives them greater opportunities when they look for work.

3 All of the opinion statements a–h below are very broad. For each statement, decide whether you agree or disagree.

a   Universities should make more links with businesses.

b   The present young generation knows more than their previous counterparts.

c   Teaching thinking at school is essential, even at primary level.

d   More time needs to be devoted to learning music, either during or after school hours.

e   Physical education is a necessary part of the learning process for all pupils.

f   Play is a major part of the learning process for children.

g   It is important for children to try to learn another language early in their education.

h   Being bored and learning to deal with boredom is a necessary part of the learning process for children.

4 Look again at the statements you agreed with in 3. Choose from the phrases below to intensify your opinions and add these to the sentences you agreed with in 3.

Example

It is important that universities should make more links with business.

| It is important that   There is no doubt that   One cannot deny that
It is impossible to argue against the fact that |

Technique

When you make an opinion statement that is very general, make sure you justify it with a reason. Use phrases such as *because* and *since* as trigger words.

5 Look again at the phrases you disagreed with in 3. It is possible to present opinions as belonging to someone else – possibly to hide your own opinion. Choose from the phrases below and add these to the sentences you disagreed with in 3.

> Some people think/feel/believe/claim/argue that
> Other people are of the opinion that
> Yet other people put forward the view that

6 To avoid overgeneralization, give reasons. Add the reasons below to opinions a–h in 3.

1 *since* it creates a healthy basis for later life.

2 *as* it helps the brain to function better and increases coordination.

3 *because* children now find it more difficult to reason.

4 *since* they have more access to information.

5 *because* it helps them intellectually and also helps to find a job.

6 *as* this would connect their research with the real world.

7 *because* interaction helps to develop social skills.

8 *as* it teaches them how to be creative on their own.

Developing reasons

7 In IELTS, opinions and reasons should be supported with 'examples from your knowledge and experience'. Sentences a–c give three examples to support the argument below. Match each example with the descriptions 1–3.

Play is a major part of the learning process for children as it teaches them how to be creative.

a Take for example children in my country who learn musical games at an early age.

b For instance, children who draw and paint are widely known to have greater spacial awareness.

c For example, play can develop artistic or musical skills.

1 a general example

2 an example from knowledge

3 an example from experience

8 Develop the ideas below by adding your own examples like those in 7 on page 35. Use the phrases in the box to help you.

> For instance,   For example,   like   namely
> Take for example   A good example is

a   Out of school activities help children develop because they can learn subjects that are not in the school curriculum.

....

....

b   Education is being reduced to a production line because the focus is on targets rather than on learning.

....

....

c   Travel helps to broaden the minds of children because it helps to bring to life the things they read in class.

....

....

d   Private education complements state education very well as it can do things state education cannot.

....

....

e   Successful entrepreneurs and sports stars should teach in schools and universities since they would provide good role models for young people.

....

....

9 Develop three of the sentences below. Use phrases to intensify your own or others' opinions. Give your own reasons and examples.

Example: Too much emphasis is put on passing exams.

Some people feel that too much emphasis is put on passing exams, *because* pupils spend a large proportion of school time doing tests rather than learning. *For example,* children in some British schools prepare for tests for weeks before the exams, *but* they are not taught anything.

a   Foreign language learning should be compulsory.

b   Students need to have good study skills on entering university.

c   University lecturers need some teacher training.

d   Boys and girls ought to be educated in separate schools.

e   Teachers' salaries need to be as high as doctors' or lawyers'.

Technique

When you state a reason, think how you could illustrate it with examples. Use phrases such as *For example* and *like* as trigger words.

Practice Test 4

Task 1

You should spend about 20 minutes on this task.

The bar chart shows the highest qualification attained by sex for the working age population in Wales in 2001/2002.

Summarize the information by selecting and reporting the main features, and make comparisons where relevant.

Write at least 150 words.

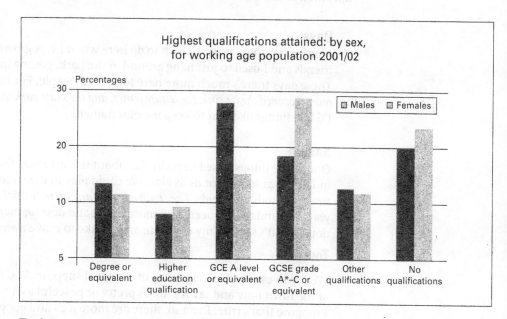

Highest qualifications attained: by sex, for working age population 2001/02

Task 2

You should spend about 40 minutes on this task.
Write about the following topic:

Some people believe that competitive sports, both team and individual, have no place in the school curriculum. How far do you agree or disagree?

Give reasons for your answer and include any relevant examples from your own knowledge or experience.
Write at least 250 words.

Youth

Unit aims

Task 1	Task 2
Describing changes	Developing and justifying opinions
Describing locations	Writing introductions

Task 1 Describing changes

1 Read the comments by three people talking about the town where they grew up. Answer the questions below.

Dave

I remember there wasn't much to do here when I was growing up. My friends and I used to just hang around in the park, getting into trouble. These days there's much more here for young people. For instance, *the council opened the ice rink, the leisure centre, and the skate park last year*. I wish I'd had things like that to keep me entertained.

Sandra

One of the things I used to really like about this area was the peace and quiet. It was so safe for us as kids. We could play in the streets or in the nearby woods and fields. *They built a bypass and an industrial estate a few years ago*, and there's been a lot more traffic and development since. I don't feel it's safe for my children, and I'd like to move away.

Tom

Well, you can't stand in the way of change, I suppose. Yes, people look at the town now and say it's not as pretty or peaceful as it was in the past. I suppose that's true. Even so, there are more jobs and opportunities now than there were when I was a teenager. I guess you can't have one without losing the other.

a For each speaker, do they think things were better or worse when they were young? Why?

b What changes have occurred to the place you come from? Do you think they are positive or negative changes?

c How could you express the phrases in italics in a more formal way?

d Imagine you are a young person moving to a new town. Which facilities in the list below would be important to you?

golf course	skate park	theatre	railway station	concert hall
gallery	stadium	ice rink	park	college	airport

2 The maps below show changes that took place in Youngsville in New Zealand over a 25-year period from 1980 to 2005. Answer the following questions:

a What is the most noticeable difference between the two maps?
b Was the town more or less residential in 2005 compared to 1980?
c Were there more or fewer trees in 2005?
d Were the changes dramatic or negligible over the 25-year period?
e What were the two biggest changes north of the river?
f What happened to the houses and trees along the railway line south of the river?

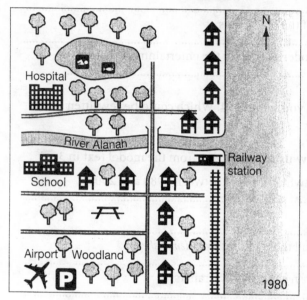

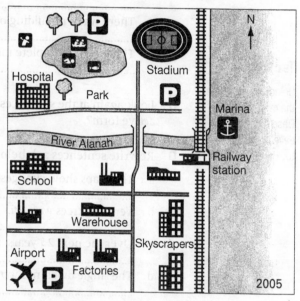

3 Complete the model text below. Use one word from the following list to complete each blank space. The first one has been done for you.

> houses   experienced   noticeable   factories   ~~developments~~
> comparison   residential   corner   facilities   construction

Model text

Technique

In order to identify changes, study the maps and number the changes on the second one. Think of some general statements, and make notes.

The maps show the ¹ _developments_ which took place in the coastal town of Youngsville between 1980 and 2005.

In 1980, the town was a much greener ² .... area with a large number of trees and individual houses, but during the next 25 years the town ³ .... a number of dramatic changes. The most ⁴ .... is that all of the trees south of the River Alanah were cut down, with all the ⁵ .... along the railway line being knocked down and replaced by skyscrapers. Moreover, a new industrial estate with ⁶ .... and warehouses

sprang up around the airport and school.

Only a few trees north of the river remained. The woodland was cleared to make way for a park, a golf course, and car parking ⁷ .... Further developments were the ⁸ .... of a stadium near the north-east ⁹ .... of the lake and a new stretch of railway from the river running directly north. A marina was also built at the mouth of the river.

Overall, a ¹⁰ .... of the two maps reveals a change from a largely rural to a mainly urban landscape.

4 Transform the sentences below by changing the nouns into verbs and using the passive. Refer to page 7 for more information on *Related verbs and nouns*.

Example

There were *spectacular changes* in the area.
The area *was changed* spectacularly.

a There were dramatic developments in the town centre.

....

b There was a complete transformation of the neighbourhood.

....

c There was a total reconstruction of the residential area.

....

d There was a total redevelopment of the old factories.

....

e There was a rebuilding of the old houses.

....

f There was a complete modernization of the entertainment district.

....

Technique

Do not just describe the map or maps. Describe the developments that took place.

5 Look again at the sentences you wrote in 4. Which could be rewritten in the active form?

6 Rewrite sentences a–h below using synonyms from the model text in 3.

a The maps show changes which *occurred* between 1980 and 2005.

....

b Very few trees *were left*.

....

c Over the next 25 years, all these houses *were demolished*.

....

d The single dwellings *were replaced* by skyscrapers.

....

e The trees *were chopped down*.

....

f The area *witnessed* dramatic changes.

....

g The woodland *gave way* to a golf course.

....

h A marina *was also constructed*.

....

7 Put the verbs below into the correct form. All of the changes took place between 2000 and 2005.

Examples

The block of flats was turned (turn) into a hotel. (passive)
The block of flats made way (make way) for a hotel. (active)

a The row of old houses .... (knock down) to make way for a road.
b The forest .... (cut down) to build a railway.
c The area .... (redevelop) completely.
d The factory .... (convert) into an art gallery.
e The city centre .... (undergo) a total transformation.
f The row of old terraced houses in the city .... (pull down) and .... (replace) by a block of flats.
g A sports complex .... (construct) in the suburbs.
h A number of spectacular changes .... (take place).
i The whole centre of the town .... (transform) by new developments.

8 Which of the following cannot be used to replace the phrase *Between 2000 and 2005*?

a   Over the period
b   During the five year period
c   From 2000 to 2005
d   Over the past five years ⊙

9 The past perfect (*had done*) can also be used to describe changes occurring before a specific time in the past. Look at the examples. Then insert *By 2005* at the beginning of each sentence in 7 and adjust each sentence.

Examples

By 2005, the block of flats *had been turned* into a hotel. (passive)
By 2005, the block of flats *had made way* for a hotel. (active)

Describing locations

10 It is sometimes important to state locations clearly on a map. Read the examples. Then answer the questions a–g about the maps on page 39 using the phrases in the box.

Example

Only a few trees *north of the river* remained.
Where is the golf course? It is *north-west of the lake*.

> south of the river   beside the railway line   in the south-west of the town
> north of the skyscrapers   south of the golf course
> south-west of the stadium   north-east of the lake

a   Where are the skyscrapers? They are ....
b   Where is the stadium? It is ....
c   Where is the lake? It is ....
d   Where is the hospital? It is ....
e   Where is the railway station? It is ....
f   Where is the airport? It is ....
g   Where is the school? It is ....

11 Complete the following sentences by choosing the correct prepositions of place from the alternatives.

a   Several changes took place *at/in/on* the town of Northgate.
b   North of the town, there is a lake surrounded *in/of/by* trees.
c   A number of new houses were built *beside/at/on* the railway line.
d   There was a large industrial area located *on/in/at* the north.
e   A new railway was constructed which ran *from/at/in* north to south.
f   Two new hotels were erected *on/in/at* the banks of the river.
g   A large number of new villas were built *beside/at/to* the sea.
h   A yachting club was set up *on/in/at* the shores of the lake.
i   A number of wind turbines were placed in the sea, just *off/on/to* the coastline.

I get better results. I should get more.

I should get paid more – I have more experience.

1 Look at the pictures and the text. Answer the questions below.

a Which person do you agree with?

b Do you agree with the justification for each person's opinion?

c Is this situation the same all over the world?

2 Read the following Task 2 question, then answer questions a–b.

Employers should pay young people the same salary as older colleagues doing the same job.

To what extent do you agree or disagree?

a Do you have to strongly agree or disagree? Is is possible to take a neutral view?

b Rewrite the statement in your own words. Begin with *Young employees ....*

3 Read a–g, taken from an answer to the question in 2. Match each sentence or part-sentence with the correct **function** from the list. The first one has been done for you.

Contradiction Explanation Result Example Reason (x 2) ~~Opinion statement~~

a Many people believe that workers should be paid according to age rather than merit.   *Opinion statement*

b . However, I feel that they should be paid according to results.   ....

c Take for example someone in their twenties working in a financial company.   ....

d They deserve to receive the same salary ...   .

e ... because they are doing the same work.   ....

f Moreover, young people nowadays are often faster at doing things than their older work colleagues ...   .

g ... which compensates for lack of experience.   ....

4   Underline the **linking phrases** in 3 which indicate the **functions** you chose.

5   Using the sentences in 3 as a model, write a paragraph expressing your own opinion in response to the question in 2. Use appropriate linking phrases.

6   Read the Task 2 question and the model answer below. For each of 1–6, two options are possible and one is incorrect. Delete the incorrect option.

> *Some people feel that young people face more pressures today than the equivalent age groups did in previous generations. Others think that they have a much easier life than their parents did. What is your opinion?*

Model text

Life for the young in today's world is in some ways certainly more comfortable than for those in previous generations. [1] *However/Moreover/Even so*, one cannot deny the fact that in a number of areas life is much more demanding than it used to be.

Take the workplace, for example. Competition for every job is now fierce in all parts of the world, not just developed countries, [2] *while/because/as* young people are more qualified than previous generations. [3] *Furthermore/Likewise/And*, there is increased mobility of people in the international job market. Skilled workers move from the Far East to Europe. India, [4] *for instance/also/in particular*, has a large pool of mobile skilled workers. This globalization of jobs has [5] *consequently/however/as a result* put intense pressure on young people as they search for work in their home countries. [6] *Thus/So/Subsequently*, it is no longer a case of just being good: young people are expected to be top rate.

7   Decide which **functions** are indicated by the correct **linking phrases** in 6.

1	a contrast	b result	c addition
2	a contrast	b reason	c result
3	a addition	b contrast	c result
4	a contrast	b addition	c example
5	a result	b contrast	c reason
6	a example	b reason	c conclusion

8 Read the statements below and in each case contradict them. Begin by using one of following expressions in the box.

> Nevertheless, I feel ...   However, I think ...
> Personally, I believe ...

Technique

When developing and justifying opinions, you do not need to tell the truth. Make a statement and use linking phrases as trigger words to think up and organize ideas.

a Many feel that young people have much more influence in the world than their counterparts in the past.

....

b According to some people, older workers are just as equipped to deal with the modern world as young people.

....

c Some people are of the opinion that advertising should not be banned in TV programmes directed at young people.

....

Writing introductions

9 Read the Task 2 questions and introductions below. Match each introduction a–c with one of the questions 1–4.

1 All forms of media but especially films and TV programmes should be censored to protect young people. To what extent do you agree?

2 The younger generation are the main driving force behind many of the latest technological developments. How far do you agree?

3 Blogs on the web are very effective ways for people to express their ideas and relieve tensions. What is your opinion?

4 The modern emphasis on computers reduces the development of any creative ability. How far do you agree?

a It is certainly important to make sure that people are protected from harmful material in various media. However, I feel that care needs to be taken in doing so for various reasons.

b In some areas, it does appear that computers reduce creativity, but I also feel they can be used as a tool to develop creative ability in many fields.

c While the youth of today definitely have an impact on the way new technology develops, there are other factors involved.

Technique

Keep your introductions short. Write only one or two sentences.

10 For the remaining title, write your own introduction. Try to paraphrase the statement in the title in one sentence, and then write another statement to show how you intend to organize your essay.

Practice Test 5

Task 1

You should spend about 20 minutes on this task.

The maps below show the changes that have taken place at the seaside resort of Templeton between 1990 and 2005.

Summarize the information by selecting and reporting the main features, and make comparisons where relevant.

Write at least 150 words.

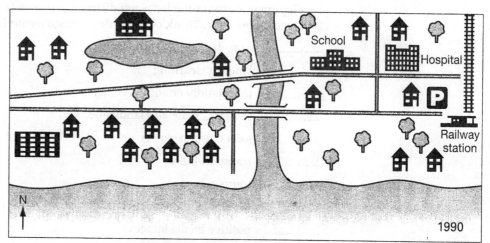

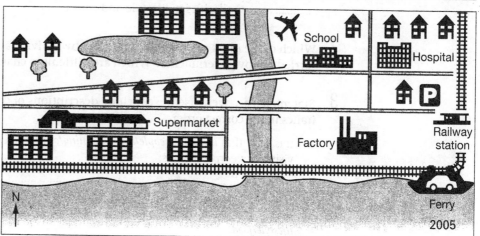

Task 2

You should spend about 40 minutes on this task.
Write about the following topic:

Young people are much more aware of and concerned about issues like the environment, poverty, and animal welfare than previous generations. What is your own opinion?

Give reasons for your answer and include any relevant examples from your own knowledge or experience.
Write at least 250 words.

Culture

Unit aims

Task 1

Concluding statements
Concession (1)

Task 2

Expressing advantages and disadvantages
Advantage and disadvantage vocabulary
Concession (2)

Task 1 Concluding statements

1 Rank the ideas in the list below 1–10 according to how important they are in developing understanding between different cultures (1 = most important; 10 = least important). Think of examples to justify your ideas.

.... organized student exchanges

.... language learning

.... international trade agreements

.... similar climate and landscape

.... joint cultural events

.... transport links

.... tourism

.... shared scientific and technological know-how

.... positive media images

.... similarities in lifestyle and culture

2 Which of the ideas in 1 can be carried out by individuals? Which can be carried out by governments? Which are difficult to change?

3 Statements a–c were used to conclude descriptions of data. Put the words in italics in the correct order.

a   It is clear that *majority/people/overwhelming/of/the/were/of/favour/in* school visits between countries.

    ....

b   Overall, just over half the people surveyed found the climate in the tropics the most difficult thing to adapt to, *a/number/with/smaller/naming/and/lifestyle/food*.

    ....

c   The three languages in question, Spanish, Arabic, and Chinese, were named as *important/the/languages/most* after English by *about/of/equal/people/numbers*.

    ....

4 Answer these questions about the sentences in 3.

a   Which topic in 1 do they relate to?

b   Which pie chart 1–4 on page 47 would be a good illustration of each concluding statement in 3? Use the proportions in each sentence to help you.

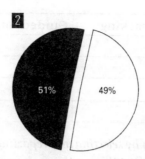
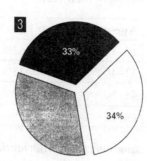
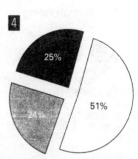

5 Pie charts are frequently used to summarize data. Therefore, they can often by used as the basis for concluding statements. Match each of the following conclusions to one of the pie charts 1–4 above.

a To conclude, only a small minority of people felt that the language barrier would prevent the development of cultural links.

b It is evident that opinions are split almost equally between the three options as regards the benefits of joint cultural ventures.

c It would seem that the vast majority of people think that the development of trade links has the greatest impact on international relations.

d Just under half the people surveyed are of the opinion that China would be the biggest cultural influence in the world by 2020.

e About half of the holiday makers visited Italy because they were interested in the art and culture, whereas the food and the climate were named as the most important factors by approximately equal numbers of the remaining tourists in the survey.

> **Technique**
>
> Aim to include several key features in your description: a paraphrase of the question, a proportion phrase, some comparison, some general and specific statements, and a concluding statement.

6 Rewrite the sentences below using a suitable phrase from the list.

nearly a third	almost equal numbers	the vast majority
a tiny minority	just under half	nearly two-thirds

Examples

Government subsidies accounted for *63 per cent of all funding.*
Government subsidies accounted for *nearly two-thirds of all funding.*

a *Eighty-seven per cent of holiday makers* to China were very satisfied with their experience.

....

b It is clear that *about 50 per cent of both sexes* favoured increased cultural contacts.

....

c Only *eleven per cent of filmgoers* thought films helped promote cultural awareness.

....

d In conclusion, the trend is clearly upward with *47 per cent of companies* establishing new trade and cultural links in 2005.

....

e To sum up, *32 per cent of all tourists* were on some form of package holiday.

....

7 Look again at the sentences in 3, 5, and 6. Make a list of phrases which are used to indicate conclusions.

The table below shows the age profile of tourists on backpacking holidays and guided tours in New Zealand in 2005, and the pie chart gives the satisfaction rating of their stay.

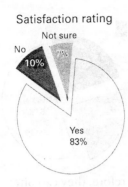

Satisfaction rating

Age profile	Backpacking	Guided tours
18–30	62%	7%
31–40	23%	22%
41–50	10%	57%
Other	5%	14%

Summarize the information by selecting and reporting the main features, and make comparisons where relevant.

8 Read the Task 1 question and answer questions a–c.

a How does the age profile of people on each holiday type differ?

b Which age group is almost equally represented on each type of holiday?

c How would you describe the opinion of the majority of visitors?

9 Complete the model text with verbs from the box. The first gap has been done for you.

comes   accounts for   belong   ~~provides~~
enjoyed   is rated   make up   include

Model text

The table [1] .provides. a breakdown by selected age group of those on backpacking and guided tours in New Zealand in 2005, with the pie chart indicating whether they [2] .... their holiday.

As can be seen from the table, the age profile of people on the two different types of holiday varies considerably. For example, the majority (62 per cent) of those on backpacking holidays [3] .... to the 18–30 age range, but the same age group [4] .... a small proportion (seven per cent) of those on guided tours. However, the pattern is the complete reverse when it

[5] .... to 41–50 year-olds. These people [6] .... 57 per cent of those on guided tours, despite accounting for only ten per cent of backpackers.

By contrast, the profiles for both backpacking and guided tours [7] .... roughly equal proportions from the 31–40 age group: 23 and 22 per cent respectively.

It is clear from the pie chart that New Zealand [8] .... as a popular holiday destination among the majority of all holiday-makers, with a massive 83 per cent from both groups stating they enjoyed their holiday.

10 Which phrase is used to indicate a concluding statement in the model text?

Concession (1)

11 Read the example sentences below. Then answer questions a–c.

Examples

Fifty-seven per cent of people on guided tours were aged 41–50, although only ten per cent of backpackers belonged to this age group.

Fifty-seven per cent of people on guided tours were aged 41–50. Nevertheless, only ten per cent of backpackers belonged to this age group.

a Which **linking phrases** are used to introduce a contrast?
b How are the phrases used differently?
c Find three examples of similar phrases in the model text in 9. Which phrases in the example sentences are they like? Which phrase can only be used before a noun or an -*ing* form?

12 Match a–e below with suitable follow-ons 1–5 to create correct statements about the data in 8.

a *Despite* accounting for nearly equal proportions of each holiday type,
b *Although* people aged 41–50 were dominant on guided tours,
c Guided tours were least popular among people in the 18–30 age group,
d One in ten people said that they didn't enjoy their holiday.
e Only fourteen per cent of people from the 'other' category chose guided tours.

1 they still accounted for one in ten backpackers.
2 *Nevertheless*, most clearly expressed satisfaction.
3 this age group still accounted for under a quarter of each.
4 *However*, that was still a higher proportion than the 18–30 age group.
5 *but* they were most popular with the oldest group.

> **Technique**
>
> Show that you can combine ideas into complex sentences.

13 Join each of the following sentences using the phrase given.

a The vast majority of visitors to Britain come from Europe. However, they stay for fewer than ten days on average.

Although ....

b Forty-five per cent of people speak a foreign language. Nevertheless, the vast majority are at a low level.

Although forty-five per cent ....

c It has good weather. However, southern France is visited by only two per cent of Asian tourists.

Despite ....

d The cost of student exchanges went up. Nevertheless, the number of exchanges rose.

The number of student exchanges ....

e The event was promoted to teenagers. Nevertheless, they accounted for only 32 per cent of the audience.

Although ....

Task 2 Expressing advantages and disadvantages

1   Look at the photos of popular electronic items. Which ideas in the box explain the popularity of each item in the pictures? What do you think the next electronic craze will be?

> size   design   portability   technology
> business need   entertainment   fashion   price

2   Read the Task 2 question below. Then answer the questions.

> *Portable entertainment devices, such as MP3 or DVD-players, which allow people to listen to music or watch films on the move, are now commonplace. What do you think are the main advantages and disadvantages of this development?*

a   Which part of the question states the general subject?
b   Which part of the question contains the **organizing words**?

3   Decide whether each idea below is an advantage or a disadvantage. Which entertainment devices would you associate them with?

a   It helps people to relax.
b   It allows people greater freedom.
c   It reduces communication.
d   It makes life more enjoyable.
e   It makes entertainment more accessible everywhere.
f   It makes people more isolated.
g   It is a nuisance for other travellers.
h   It makes people less sociable.

4   Complete each sentence a–f with a word from the box.

> help   difficult   interfere   benefits   ideal   enable

a   These devices bring a number of ....
b   The main one, in my opinion, is that they .... people relax, for example, while they are studying or working in cafes or on trains.
c   Some people find it .... to do so when it is completely quiet outside their homes.
d   So these devices .... people to relax and create a familiar environment.
e   Sometimes, however, they do .... with others if the volume is too high, hence the quiet zones in many trains.
f   Nevertheless, laptops, etc are .... , because they allow people to ao things where they want to rather than being restricted to working at home.

5   Decide whether the words in 4 express advantage or disadvantage.

6   The sentences in 4 form a paragraph taken from an answer to the Task 2 question. Answer questions a–c.

a   Which sentence in 4 expresses a disadvantage?
b   Which **linking phrases** are used in 4?
c   Which ideas from 3 are used in the paragraph?

از فروشگاه ما دیدن فرمایید...

7 The paragraph below is taken from a similar answer. Complete the paragraph with words from the box.

> even if   likewise   for example   though
> consequently   and   although

> The main drawback is, in my opinion, quite obvious. Take [1].................
> people of all ages who are travelling on trains nowadays. [2]................. they
> are reading, they are plugged into the radio, talking on their mobiles, or
> listening to music on their MP3-players. [3]................. , others are playing
> games, watching a film, and working simultaneously, even [4].................
> they have friends next to them to talk to. [5]................. this allows people
> greater freedom and flexibility [6]................. takes away the boredom of
> journeys, people are becoming more and more isolated in their own
> worlds. [7]................. , the art of communication is being lost.

8 Answer these questions about the paragraph in 7.

a   Does this paragraph concentrate on an advantage or a disadvantage?
b   Which ideas does this paragraph mention from the list in 3 on page 50?
c   Underline the main advantage and disadvantage in the paragraph.

Advantage and disadvantage vocabulary

9 Nouns can be used to express advantage and disadvantage. Complete sentences a–g with words from the box.

> benefit   problems   opportunities   chance
> handicap   drawbacks   gain

a   Not knowing a foreign language has its .... , such as when one tries
    to make contact with people in other countries.

b   Visiting other countries gives people a .... to experience cultures first
    hand.

c   The financial .... to any nation exceeds all other benefits.

d   If people take time to find out about the country they are travelling to, they
    will face fewer ....

e   These days not having access to the web to find out what is going on is a
    serious ....

f   Cultural exchanges offer enormous .... to the nations involved.

g   Being culturally aware is of great .... in business.

10 Adjectives can also be used to emphasize advantage and disadvantage. Does the word *serious* in 9e emphasize advantage or disadvantage?

Technique

Use nouns, verbs and adjectives, such as *benefit* and *drawback*, which express advantages and disadvantages as trigger words to help you plan.

11 Decide whether each adjective in the box expresses advantage or disadvantage.

> ~~advantageous~~   beneficial   useful   worthless
> invaluable   difficult   helpful   convenient

Advantage: ___advantageous___

Disadvantage: ....

12 Write the opposite of each of the adjectives in 11. Where possible, add or remove a prefix or suffix to create the opposite.

Example

advantageous   ___disadvantageous___

13 Verbs can also indicate advantages and disadvantages. Complete the following sentences in your own words.

a   International arts festivals *encourage* ....

b   Lending artworks to other countries *improves* ....

c   Films and concerts *enhance* ....

d   To *enable* children to value their heritage, ...

e   Personal links can *benefit* ....

f   Ignorance of other people's traditions can *handicap* ....

g   To *prevent* countries falling out with each other, ...

Concession (2)

14 Read sentences 1 and 2 and answer the questions a and b.

1   Although the vast majority of electronic devices are very useful, they are also highly annoying.

2   Despite being highly annoying, the vast majority of electronic gadgets are very useful.

a   Which word introduces the concession in each case?

b   Which sentence emphasizes the advantage? Which emphasizes the disadvantage?

15 Complete sentences a–e with words from the box.

> nevertheless   however   despite   although   but

a   .... listening to music on CDs is very pleasant, it is not as good as a live concert.

b   Documentaries are invaluable sources of knowledge. .... , they need to be entertaining as well as informative.

c   .... the large numbers of tourists, ancient buildings and temples are still inspiring places to visit.

d   Sculptures can make gardens and public spaces attractive. .... , they are expensive to look after.

e   Arts exhibitions show the public artefacts they would not normally see, ... at a price.

Practice Test 6

Task 1

You should spend about 20 minutes on this task.

The table below shows how young people in Tokyo, Japan, listened to music over the previous month. The pie chart shows a record company's international findings about whether people preferred live or recorded music.

Summarize the information by selecting and reporting the main features, and make comparisons where relevant.

Write at least 150 words.

	Live music	MP3-players	Internet	CDs
Male	60%	79%	55%	19%
Female	44%	40%	42%	22%

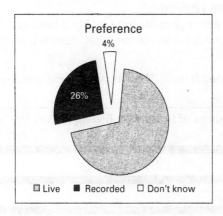

Task 2

You should spend about 40 minutes on this task.
Write about the following topic:

It is important for travellers and business people to understand the cultures they come into contact with, however briefly. What are the main advantages of doing so? What do you think is the main disadvantage of not doing so?

Give reasons for your answer and include any relevant examples from your own knowledge or experience.
Write at least 250 words.

Unit aims

Task 1	Task 2
Adverbs	Discussing other people's opinions
Using adverbs to evaluate data	Hypothesizing
Avoiding irrelevance	

Task 1 Adverbs

1 Read these conflicting views about scientists moving to rich countries.
Answer questions a–c.

The 'brain drain' of skilled workers like scientists and technicians to rich
economies is morally wrong.
People should have greater freedom to work where they want. Surely, it's a
personal matter.

a Which views do you agree with?
b Is this 'brain drain' a new phenomenon, or has it been around for a long time?
c Should something be done about the situation or is it unstoppable?

2 Read the Task 1 question below. Then answer questions a–e.

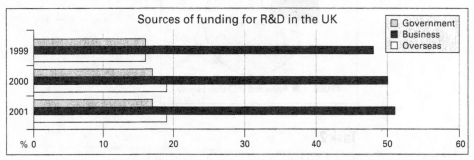

*The chart above shows sources of funding for research and development (R&D)
in the UK from 1999 to 2001. The table below shows the percentage of national
income spent on R&D for a range of countries.*

Proportion of national income allocated to R&D (1999)						
UK	USA	Germany	France	Italy	Japan	EU average
1.82%	2.75%	2.4%	2.3%	1.1%	2.9%	1.81%

*Summarize the information by selecting and reporting the main features, and
make comparisons where relevant.*

a What general trend can you see in the chart?
b What general pattern can you see in the table?
c Which is clearly the main source of funding in the bar chart?
d Which piece of data in the table can you use as a standard for comparison?
e Which pieces of information in the table are significant?

3 Complete the model text below with verbs from the box.

> rose   contributed (x 2)   was   overtook
> was spent   is shown   came   ~~shows~~

Model text

The chart [1] ..shows.. information about the main sources of funding for scientific research and development (R&D) in the UK. The proportion of national income spent on R&D by country [2] .... in the table.

Between 1999 and 2001, the amount of funding allocated from each source [3] .... very slightly. Approximately half of all investment throughout the period [4] .... from business, while the government consistently [5] .... around seventeen per cent. It is also noticeable that in eighteen of 1999 overseas spending on R&D in the UK was comparable to the government's, at around seventeen per cent. But for the last two years it [6] .... government spending in this area.

As regards the proportion of national income allocated to R&D, the highest percentage (2.9 per cent) [7] .... by Japan, followed closely by the USA (2.5 per cent). By contrast, Italy [8] .... the smallest amount of national income to R&D, only 1.1 per cent, significantly below the EU average of 1.81 per cent.

It is interesting to note that although the UK's spending on R&D [9] .... above the EU average in 1999, it is considerably behind other close trading partners France and Germany.

4 Find examples of adverbs ending in -ly used in the model text.

5 Choose the most suitable adverb in sentences a–h.

Examples

The trend for other countries was *completely/~~well~~* different.
Government investment rose *significantly/~~highly~~*.

a The government's spending for the past year was *significantly/well* higher than before.
b Women have been *consistently/deeply* under-represented in science jobs.
c Workers in *highly/lowly/considerably* paid jobs are generally healthier.
d The company's sales are *slightly/much* behind its competitors.
e Sales were *marginally/deeply* up on the previous quarter.
f Investment in the arts rose quite *considerably/slightly/seriously*.
g *Slightly/Approximately/Well* half the spending was from the private sector.
h The income for the arts centre was *substantially/much/highly* down on the previous year.

6 Match the adverbs a–g below with their opposites 1–7.

a	well	1	rapidly
b	marginally	2	slightly
c	approximately	3	exactly
d	constantly	4	badly
e	slowly	5	considerably
f	significantly	6	partially
g	completely	7	erratically

Using adverbs to evaluate data

7 Look again at the model text in **3** on page 55. Which phrases are used to introduce sentences instead of *noticeably* and *interestingly*?

8 Rewrite each sentence a–h using an adverb or starting with *It*.

Example

Clearly, the trend is upward.
It is clear that the trend is upward.

a   It is significant that the number of scientists per head of population has declined in recent years.

....

b   Interestingly, the sales failed to recover.

It ....

c   It is probable that numbers will continue to fall over the period.

....

d   It is not surprising that there were skills shortages in the chemical industry.

....

e   Evidently, investment needs to be increased.

It ....

f   Noticeably, the pattern for investment in the arts is the reverse.

It ....

g   More importantly, the cost of plasma screens is set to fall.

It ....

h   Not surprisingly, analogue TV sales then fell.

It ....

9 Different adverbs can be put in different places in sentences. Which sentences a–d are possible?

a   *Considerably*, sales fell.
b   Sales fell *considerably*.
c   *Clearly*, the trend was downward.
d   The trend was *clearly* downward.

10 Put the adverb in brackets in the correct place in the sentence. Some can be used in more than one place.

a   The number of science graduates fell. (significantly)
b   The number of technical staff in hospitals is falling. (evidently)
c   The cost of training scientists is increasing year by year. (noticeably)
d   Investment in capital equipment like specialist machinery is down on last year. (interestingly)
e   Sales of new televisions soared before the World Cup. (not surprisingly)
f   The trend is now upward. (obviously)

> **Technique**
> Use at least one adverb or adverbial phrase to help you evaluate the data.

11 Write your own sentences about the data in **2** on page 54.

a   Describe the bar chart, using *marginally*, *approximately*, and *slowly*.
b   Describe the table, using *considerably*, *evidently*, *noticeably*, *slightly*, and *interestingly*.

Avoiding irrelevance

12 Look at the chart below, which shows how students on all courses at an Australian university viewed different subjects on a scale of easy to difficult. Answer questions a–f.

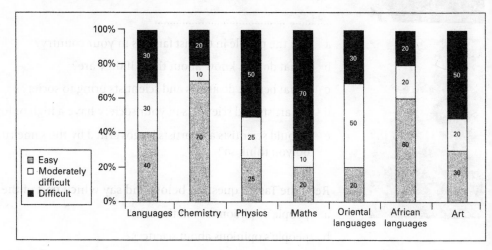

a Whose opinions does the chart show?

b How many subjects does the chart show?

c Which subject was rated as 'difficult' by the highest percentage of students?

d Which other subjects were judged 'difficult' or 'moderately difficult' by a large number (over 70 per cent) of students?

e Which subject was rated as 'easy' by the highest percentage of students?

f Is there a clear correspondence between the type of subject and whether it was rated as easy or difficult? Give examples to show why/why not.

Technique

Do not speculate when you describe data unless you are asked to. Avoid writing lists of detail.

13 Decide whether the statements a–f are relevant or irrelevant, and explain why. Irrelevant statements may contain an unnecessary opinion, too much data, or unnecessary speculation.

a The subject which was rated as difficult by the highest percentage of students (70 per cent) was mathematics, mainly because I think it is complex for many students.

b By contrast, the subject which was most often judged as easy was chemistry.

c The chart shows the opinions of Australian students on whether different subjects were easy or difficult.

d African languages were seen as easy, which is somewhat surprising when you consider the range of languages in Africa.

e Oriental languages were ranked as easy by only about 20 per cent.

f The Y axis shows the percentages, and the bars contain the numbers about the legend at the bottom.

14 Describe the chart in 12 in your own words.

Task 2 Discussing other people's opinions

1 Complete the list below with a famous artist and scientist from your country.

Leonardo da Vinci
Albert Einstein
Sir Isaac Newton
Nicolaus Copernicus

....

....

  a Are the people in the list famous in your country?

  b What do you know about them if they are?

  c What benefit do artists and scientists bring to society?

  d Do artists and scientists in your society have a high or low status?

  e Should scientists and artists be governed by the same rules as we are? Why do you think so?

2 Read the Task 2 question below and say which part of the question relates to:

  a people's opinions about the arts?

  b people's opinions about sciences?

  c your opinion?

> *Some people believe that the arts should receive subsidies or sponsorship from government and big companies. Others feel such spending is a luxury and that it would be better if it were invested in scientific projects. Discuss both views and give your own opinion.*

3 Complete the paragraph with sentences a–c.

  a So supporters of arts groups feel that the company's travel and accommodation costs ought to receive more subsidies or sponsorship.

  b Touring theatre groups or dance companies are a case in point.

  c Many people feel strongly that arts projects like exhibitions of photography, sculpture, or paintings should be helped financially by government and big companies.

> ¹ .... They argue that such projects enrich people's lives, often simply because they are new and show a different way of doing things.
> ² .... National companies, for example, can take plays to provincial areas that don't have their own facilities. This, however, requires a lot of money. ³ .... If this were done more by the government and commercial organizations, then the arts could be brought to a wider public.

4 Which phrases are used in the paragraph in 3 to indicate someone else's opinion?

5 Match the statements a–h with the best explanations 1–8.

Example: a 4

a Amateur arts groups should be encouraged.

b The wealth of a nation is connected with scientific development.

c Science is now playing a more important role in our lives than in the past.

d The work of artists should be censored.

e Scientists should have some involvement with artists, and vice versa.

f Science is dull and boring.

g Many scientific experiments are dangerous to society.

h The work of scientists should not be tightly regulated by society.

1 Modern economies cannot advance without a strong scientific base.

2 Bringing these two groups together would be better for society as a whole.

3 It has an effect on everything we do from eating to travelling.

4 Such groups help to develop talent and bring people together.

5 Certain works of art that are produced are offensive and should be banned.

6 By limiting scientific work, we might stop certain beneficial developments.

7 There are many examples where serious mistakes have been made.

8 Spending time alone in laboratories without much human contact is not very interesting.

6 It is often useful to suggest that an opinion belongs to someone else. Read the example and phrases in the lists below. Then join your answers to 5 with similar phrases.

Example

Some people think that amateur arts groups should be encouraged. *They argue that* such groups help to develop talent and bring people together.

It is argued by some people that
Yet others believe that
Many people think that
A commonly held belief is that
Some people feel that

They claim that
They feel that
They maintain that
They argue that

7 Use the expressions in the box below to develop the explanations in 5.

Example

They argue that such groups help to develop talent and bring people together. *A good example here is* where a young artist joins a local group and progresses on to TV work.

For example,   For instance,   A case in point is … , which
A very good example here is   Take … for example. It/They

Hypothesizing

8 Match the sentence halves a–e with the endings 1–5.

a Personally, I would argue that science need not be

b However, it *could* possibly be a requirement for the first two or three years,

c During this time, children can do exciting experiments,

d If trips to places of scientific interest are also arranged,

e Above all, I think it is better for science classes to be optional

1 this *might* motivate some children to take up a science subject.

2 obligatory at this level.

3 because not all pupils are good at such subjects and any compulsion *might* discourage them.

4 like making basic chemical compounds or collecting plants.

5 as it *would* give pupils a taster.

9 The sentences in 8 form a paragraph. Why has the writer chosen to use words such as *would*, *could*, and *might*? Which sentence asks the reader to imagine a situation and its consequence?

Technique

Use linking phrases like *if* and *unless* in answer to Task 2 questions in order to hypothesize about effects.

10 The linking phrases *if*, *providing*, *provided*, and *unless* can all be used to hypothesize. Read the example. Then rewrite sentences a–d using the word given.

Example

A nation should nurture the talents of its people. It will then reap many benefits.

If *a nation nurtures the talents of its people, it will reap many benefits.*

a Without being encouraged by parents and teachers, budding musicians will not develop.

Unless ....

b Science may one day stop the ageing process in humans, but will this benefit mankind?

If .... ?

c If there is no effort to keep traditional crafts alive, they will disappear.

Unless ....

d If innovation is encouraged, many new jobs will be created.

Providing ....

11 Complete the following sentences using your own ideas.

a Provided parents have an interest in music,

....

b If government support for arts projects is not available,

....

c Unless entrance to museums and art galleries is free,

....

d Providing young scientists are given the right opportunities,

....

Practice Test 7

Task 1

You should spend about 20 minutes on this task.

The charts below show how selected age groups puchased concert, cinema, and theatre tickets online over the first three months of 2006 in three countries and how the Internet was accessed.

Summarize the information by selecting and reporting the main features, and make comparisons where relevant.

Write at least 150 words.

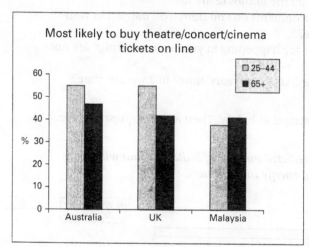

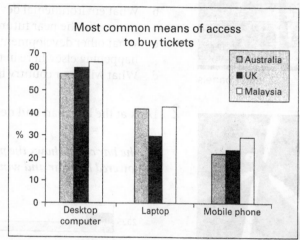

Task 2

You should spend about 40 minutes on this task.
Write about the following topic:

The money spent on space research has brought enormous benefits to mankind, but it could be more usefully applied. How far do you agree?

Give reasons for your answer and include any relevant examples from your own knowledge or experience.
Write at least 250 words.

Nature

Unit aims	
Task 1	Task 2
Making predictions	Articles
Factual accuracy	Writing conclusions

Task 1 Making predictions

1 Answer questions a–d.

a   What aspect of the future do the photos relate to?

b   What environmental developments do you think will happen in your country in the near future?

c   What other developments are happening in your country which are not happening elsewhere in the world?

d   What will your country be like in ten years' time? in 25 years' time?

solar panels

2 Look at the bar chart and description below. Then answer questions a–c.

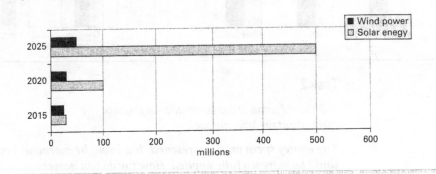

The bar chart shows the predicted number of buildings that will be powered by solar and wind energy in the future.

wind turbine

a   What does the chart show?

b   What do the numbers relate to?

c   What is the range of the numbers along the bottom of the chart?

3 The structure *will* + infinitive or a range of prediction verbs are used to talk about future statistics. Complete sentences a–d with the words *will*, *prediction* or *predicted*.

a   The number of solar-powered buildings .... increase to 500 million in 2025.

b   It is .... that the number of solar-powered buildings .... increase in the future.

c   The .... is that the number of buildings powered by solar energy .... increase.

d   The number is .... to increase to 500 million in 2025.

Technique

Before you start writing make a list of 'predict' verbs to use as trigger words.

4 Answer these questions about the sentences in 3.

    a   Which of these words could replace the word *prediction*?

projection   assumption   forecast   anticipation

    b   Which of these words could replace the word *predicted*?

projected   anticipated   forecast   said

    c   Which other words do you know to replace *prediction* and *predicted*?

5 Complete sentences a–h with the correct forms of the verbs in brackets.

    a   It .... (predict) that in 2025, solar energy .... (provide) energy for 500 million buildings worldwide.

    b   In 2015, about 25 million buildings .... (expect) to receive energy from wind power.

    c   In 2025, much more energy to power buildings .... (come) from solar energy compared to wind power.

    d   In the future, solar energy .... (forecast) to be a much greater source of energy than wind power.

    e   In the future, wind power .... (not expect) to be as great a source of power as solar energy.

    f   In years to come, it .... (project) that wind power .... (be) a less important source of energy than solar energy.

    g   Solar energy .... (set) to assume greater importance as a source of energy in the future.

    h   In 2015, it .... (anticipate) that solar energy and wind power each .... (provide) approximately the same amount of energy.

6 Which of the sentences below describes something which will happen before a future time? Which describes something in progress at a time in the future?

    a   By 2025, 500 million buildings *will have converted* to solar power. (*will have* + past participle)

    b   In/By 2025, 500 million buildings *will be using* solar power. (*will be* + *-ing* form)

7 Complete sentences a–e with the correct form of the verbs in brackets. Use *will* + infinitive, *will have* + past participle, or *will be* + *-ing* form. You may also need to use the passive.

    a   By 2020, it is expected that 30 million buildings .... (use) wind power.

    b   By 2025, very few people .... (live) in the countryside.

    c   In 2010, more bicycles .... (sell).

    d   By 2020, it is predicted that many animals .... (become) extinct.

    e   By the year 2015, it is anticipated that many natural habitats .... (destroy).

Factual accuracy

8 Look at the charts. Then answer questions a–f.

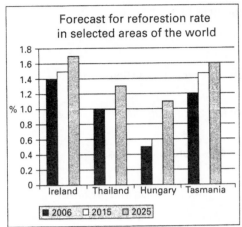

Forecast for reforestion rate in selected areas of the world
■ 2006 □ 2015 □ 2025

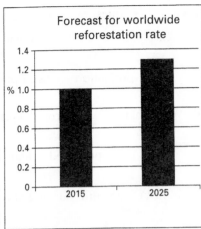

Forecast for worldwide reforestation rate

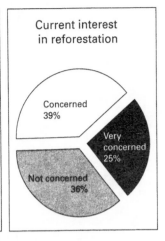

Current interest in reforestation

Concerned 39%
Very concerned 25%
Not concerned 36%

a   Which chart provides more general information? Which chart can be used for the conclusion?

b   In general, is the reforestation projected to increase or decrease?

c   Which region is projected to have the highest rate?

d   For which region does the chart show the greatest difference between 2006 and 2025?

e   Which chart contains information which could be used for a conclusion?

f   In general, are most people concerned about reforestation or not?

9 Find and correct six factual errors in the text below.

The charts show forecasts for the annual deforestation rate in selected regions and worldwide together with the current attitude towards concern for tree loss.

Generally, it forecast that the reforestation rate in the four regions will grow until 2035, though at varying rates. It is projected that Ireland will have the highest rate in 2025 at 1.5 per cent followed closely by Tasmania. The forecast for both regions for 2015 is the same at 1.5 per cent. Hungary, by contrast, with the lowest projected rate throughout the period, will experience the greatest overall increase. It is anticipated that the figure will climb from 0.5 per cent in 2015 to 0.6 per cent and then rise more sharply to 1.1 per cent.

It also worth noting that the reforestation rate in Thailand is anticipated to be exactly in line with the worldwide average for both 2015 and 2025, 1.3 per cent and 1.0 per cent respectively. Meanwhile, Hungary will be below the international rates, while both Ireland and Tasmania will exceed them.

From the pie chart, can be seen that there is some obvious concern about the need for planting more trees ('concerned' 39 per cent, and 'not very concerned' 25 per cent), while at the same time there is a sizeable proportion of people who are not concerned.

10 In each of sentences a–f there is a word missing. Add the missing word.

a   It predicted that the use of solar energy will become more important.

b   We see from the chart that largest amount of money was spent on the water conservation project.

c   The chart shows the different types of trees are found in different regions.

d   From the pie chart, can be seen that hydroelectric power constitutes seven per cent of the world energy demand.

e   It is clear that majority of people are very concerned about climate change.

f   Recently, a number of campaigns have encouraged people plant trees.

11 Look again at the text in 9. There is a missing word in each of the last three paragraphs. Add the missing words in the correct places.

12 Read the table, which describes in thousands the estimated and actual numbers of houses built in the UK by region in 2002. Answer questions a–h to identify the correct facts.

Regions	Actual	Estimated
Scotland	3,000	3,200
Northern Ireland	5,000	2,500
Wales	6,300	2,900
North of England	13,500	9,300
Central England	16,200	8,100
Southern England (exc. London)	77,500	51,100
London	47,800	24,800

a   What information does the table give?

b   How many regions of the UK is it divided into?

c   Usually, was the estimated number above or below the actual number?

d   In which three regions were the highest numbers of houses built? How did the figures for these regions compare with the estimates?

e   Which region had a disparity of just over four thousand between the estimate and the actual figure? What were the figures for this region?

f   Which other two regions followed the usual trend? What were the figures for these two regions?

g   In which region was the lowest number of houses built?

h   Which region is an exception to the general trend? What were the figures for this region?

13 Using the facts identified in your answers to the questions above, summarize the table by selecting and reporting the main features, and make comparisons where relevant. Write at least 150 words.

Task 2 Articles

1 Answer questions a–d.

  a What are the most serious threats that the natural world is facing in the twenty-first century?

  b What is the most serious threat to the environment in your country?

  c What action is being taken?

  d What further steps do you think could be taken?

2 The paragraph below has been taken from an essay on measures to reduce river pollution throughout the world. Complete the gaps with the nouns in the box. The first one has been done for you.

> factories   pollutants   action   fish   wildlife
> ~~problem~~   leisure   incentives   pressure

By far the best way to solve the ¹ problem of water pollution is to locate all ² .... away from rivers and lakes and to install waste treatment centers. All the ³ .... in the water would then be destroyed, as has been done in many old industrial areas in Poland and Germany. This would mean that ⁴ .... and ⁵ .... would be able to return to rivers and people would be able to use them for ⁶ .... like swimming and fishing. There is considerable ⁷ .... on many poor countries to develop their economies and so it would be difficult to persuade many of them to change their policies. However, I think that ⁸ .... needs to be taken and perhaps financial ⁹ .... from richer countries would help.

3 Are the words in the list below countable or uncountable?

> animal   information   nature   climate   accommodation
> knowledge   research   weather   tree   idea   situation   fact

4 Look again at the paragraph in 2. Are the answers countable or uncountable?

5 Add *a/an*, *the*, or no article to sentences a–h.

Examples

  The plastic bottles that I threw out yesterday have been taken away for recycling.

Plastic bottles are now being made of .... biodegradable materials. (no article)

  a .... knowledge about the environment can be found in .... books and on the Internet.

  b .... energy can be generated from bio-fuels.

  c Trees help to protect .... soil by conserving water.

  d Newspapers now use .... high percentage of .... recycled paper.

  e Looking after .... nature is important for all of us.

  f It is better to see animals in .... wild than in captivity.

  g .... solution to the problem is to fine people for dropping .... rubbish.

  h .... new plastic containers which I bought last week are not harmful for the environment as they are biodegradable.

6 In each text a–f, there is one mistake relating to articles. Correct the mistakes by adding or deleting a word.

Example

Animals like chimpanzees and apes should not be used for ~~the~~ experiments.

a Wave power technology is the best answer to the problem of pollution. However, the introduction of such technology also creates the problem.

b Governments worldwide should tax the cars more. A measure like this would make people think more about nature.

c In near future, houses will be more energy-efficient than they are now.

d Food industry could pay for recycled bottles as was done in the past. The bottles would then not be thrown away.

e Insects like the bees, for example, play a vital role in most ecosystems. The bee pollinates plants and flowers.

f The facilities like dams and forests are also used for leisure.

Writing conclusions

7 Read the two Task 2 questions. Then decide which question each sentence a–g relates to. Write 1 or 2 next to each sentence.

> *1 Pollution from aircraft is one of the main factors responsible for global warming. What measures could be taken to reduce this source of climate change?*

> *2 When a country becomes richer, the natural environment will suffer. It is not possible for a country to both develop its economy and protect the environment. To what extent do you agree or disagree?*

a This means that in the short term we will just have to accept paying higher prices for flights and travelling less.

b <u>In conclusion,</u> <u>I do not agree</u> that developing a country's economy has to involve destroying the natural world.

c If this type of eco-friendly business is encouraged, then there is no reason why a healthy economy and a healthy environment cannot exist together.

d <u>All in all,</u> <u>I feel that</u> imposing higher taxes on airlines is unavoidable.

e It is true that some businesses move into new areas with no regard for their effect on the environment.

f We can <u>certainly</u> investigate ways of making aircraft technology cleaner, but we do not know how long they will take to develop.

g However, there are many examples of local businesses which depend on and support the local environment.

8 A conclusion needs to state your opinion or your most important idea, and remind the reader of how you argued in favour of it. The sentences in 7 on page 67 form concluding paragraphs to the exam question. Write out the two paragraphs with the sentences in the best order, following the frameworks below.

Question 1

Statement of most important measure:

....

Another possible measure and why it is less effective:

....

Restatement of most important measure and its consequences:

....

Question 2

Statement of opinion:

....

Reference to the opposite view:

....

Technique

Always write a conclusion to your answer. Avoid repeating words in your conclusion.

Reason against the opposite view:

....

Restatement of opinion:

....

9 Look at the underlined phrases in the sentences in 7. For each one, choose two alternatives with a similar meaning from the box below.

| to sum up | I believe | of course | I would argue that | in general |

10 Your conclusion must be clear but you need to avoid making claims that sound too strong. One way to avoid this is to talk about possibilities using the phrase *There is no reason why* + negative. Read the example. Then change sentences a–d in a similar way.

Example

A healthy economy and a healthy environment can exist together.
There is no reason why a healthy economy and a healthy environment *cannot* exist together.

a   Local eco-friendly businesses can be successful.

....

b   People could take more holidays at home instead of always flying abroad.

....

c   People could travel by fast train instead of taking short flights.

....

d   Governments should give special financial support to eco-friendly business people.

....

Task 1

You should spend about 20 minutes on this task.

The table below shows the projected costings over the next five years in American dollars for three environmental projects for sustainable forestry. The pie chart shows the expected expenditure breakdown allocation for the first year as the projects are set up.

Summarize the information by selecting and reporting the main features, and make comparisons where relevant.

Write at least 150 words.

	Year 1	Year 2	Year 3	Year 4	Year 5
West Africa	10.5 million	7.5 million	2.5 million	2.5 million	3.5 million
Central America	20 million	12 million	5 million	5 million	5 million
South-east Asia	30 million	20 million	40 million	50 million	50 million

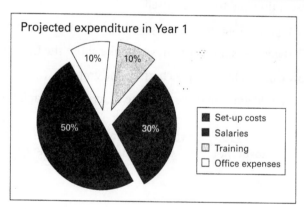

Task 2

You should spend about 40 minutes on this task.
Write about the following topic:

More and more city workers are deciding to live in the country and travel into work every day. The result is increased traffic congestion and damage to the environment.

What measures do you think could be taken to encourage people not to travel such long distances into work?

Give reasons for your answer and include any relevant examples from your own knowledge or experience.
Write at least 250 words.

Health

Unit aims

Task 1

Varying vocabulary
Checking spelling

Task 2

Organizing words
Verb-subject agreement

Task 1 Varying vocabulary

1 Answer these questions about hospitals and health care.

  a What are the main priorities of health care in your country?

  b How is health care delivered in your home country? If you want to consult a doctor, what do you do?

  c Are medicines free or do you have to pay for them?

  d What effect has technology had on medical care in your country?

2 Read the Task 1 question on page 71. Then answer questions a–e below.

  a What general statement can you make about the whole graph? Look at the description and the graph itself.

  b What general statement can you make about the French hospital?

  c What general statement can you make about the Ukrainian hospital?

  d How can you link the pie charts to the graph?

  e How could you use these words to describe the graph?

> trend   upward   similar pattern   reach a peak
> except that   saw a continuous rise   change   coincide

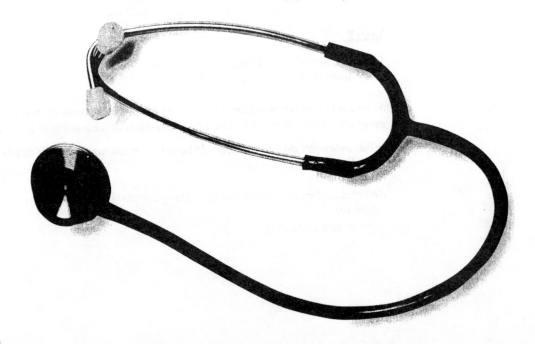

The charts below show the average bed use in three typical hospitals internationally and the proportion of hospital budgets allocated to in-patient care before and after day-surgery was introduced in 2003.

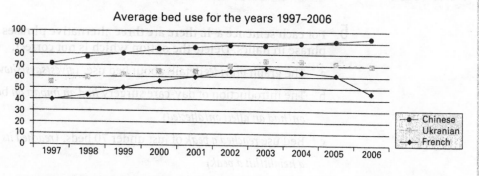

Average bed use for the years 1997–2006

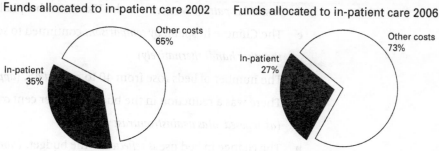

Funds allocated to in-patient care 2002

Funds allocated to in-patient care 2006

Summarize the information by selecting and reporting the main features, and make comparisons where relevant.

3 Complete the text with words from the box. The first gap has been done for you.

| peak | impact | clear | occupancy | trend | ~~details~~ |
| marked | reduction | falling | significantly | rise | experienced |

Model text

The graph provides [1] _details_ about the average beds in use each year in three similar hospitals before and after the introduction of day-care surgery.

Day-care surgery seems to have had an [2] .... on bed use in all three hospitals. At the French hospital, the figures show an upward [3] .... over the period from 40 beds to 46. However, in 2003 bed [4] .... had reached a [5] .... of just under 70 beds, before [6] .... back. A similar pattern was repeated for the Ukrainian hospital, except that the decline in bed use after 2003 was not so [7] .... (76 beds in 2003 as against 71 in 2006).

The Chinese hospital, by comparison, [8] .... a continual [9] .... in bed use between 1997 and 2006, 71 and 93 respectively. However, we see that after 2004 the rate of increase was [10] .... slower than in previous years.

It is [11] .... that the fall in bed use coincides with the [12] .... in the average budget at the three hospitals for in-patient care (35 per cent compared to 27 per cent) between 2002 and 2006.

Technique

Use a variety of alternative expressions when writing your answer to avoid repetition.

4 Look again at the words in the gaps in 3 on page 72 and choose an alternative for each one from the box. You will not use all the words.

effect	use	tendency	cut	considerably	low	evident
increase	decrease	dropping	information	result		
saw	high point	sharp	dramatically			

5 For each sentence a–h, there are three alternative phrases to replace the phrase in italics. Delete the option which is not correct.

a   The graph *provides* details about bed use. (*gives/says/shows*)

b   The introduction of day-care surgery *had an impact on* bed use. (*had an effect on/had an affect on/affected*)

c   Bed use *reached a peak* of just under 70 beds. (*reached its highest point/reached a height/hit a peak*)

d   A similar *pattern* was seen in the Ukrainian hospital. (*design/trend/movement*)

e   The Chinese hospital, *by comparison*, continued to see a rise. (*by contrast/on the other hand/alternatively*)

f   The number of beds rose from 40 to *around* 45. (*approximately/about/towards*)

g   There was a reduction in the budget (35 per cent *compared to* 27 per cent). (*as opposed to/as against/contrast with*)

h   The change in bed use *is reflected in* the budget. (*can be seen in/can be viewed in/can be detected in*)

6 The descriptions below summarize the sentence structure of the model in 3. Number the notes in the correct order, based on the sentences in the model. The first and last have been done for you.

a   General introductory statement. 1

b   General statement of first main trend, then specific data. ....

c   General statement about a reinforcing trend, then specific data. ....

d   Specific statement qualifying the trend, without detail. ....

e   General statement about the line graph. ....

f   General statement of contrasting trend, then specific data. ....

g   Specific statement qualifying the trend, with detail. ....

h   General conclusion based on pie charts. 8

Checking spelling

7 In each group of four words, circle the one which is spelt incorrectly and correct it.

a	therefore	opposite	befor	limit
b	believe	achieve	recieve	brief
c	staying	stayed	studing	studied
d	usefull	helpful	hopefully	carefully
e	personaly	practical	usually	normal
f	efficient	sufficent	ancient	deficient
g	unfortunately	improvement	definitly	management
h	comfortable	diffrent	temperature	interested
i	choise	price	increase	advice
j	preferred	committed	refered	happened

8 Look again at your answers in 7. Some of the spellings depend on simple rules. What spelling rules explain the misspelt words? Compare your ideas with the key on page 110.

9 Find and correct the spelling mistakes in the following sentences. One of the sentences has two spelling mistakes.

a The numbers declined gradualy and stood at just twenty in 2006.

b In-patient care took up 25 per cent of the funds, wich was an increase of six per cent on the previous year.

c A number of significant changes occured in the following twenty years.

d The percentage increased sharply and reached a pick in 2003.

e The figres rose from approximatly 45,000 to 49,000 over the period.

• f Patient numbers rose steadily for the first ten years, and then flactuated around 500 for the following decade.

g The required number of beds exeeded what was anticipated for that year.

h Most people in the servey thought that more money should be spent on the health service.

10 Read the following extract written by an IELTS student on the number of traffic accident victims seen at a local hospital. Find the eight mistakes that he made.

> The averag number of road traffic acidents from cars increased dramaticaly between 1995 and the year 2000, rising from a total of 53 to 178 respectively. Over the next five years, there was a noticeable improvment as numbers fell steadilly to a new low point of 37 in 2006. As regard motorcycl accidents, however, it is clear the trend is upward, with more occuring in this category in the later period.

Task 2 Organizing words

1 Which of the following do you think are most important for good health?
Rank them in order of importance (1 = most important; 6 = least important).
Are there any other lifestyle factors which are not included in the list?

> taking regular exercise   carefully monitoring your diet
> having a wide range of interests   having a wide network of friends
> living in the countryside   sleeping at least seven hours a night

2 Complete the paragraph by choosing the best adverb in each case.

The [1] *normally/outlandishly/strangely* beneficial effect that animals have on people's health and general well-being is now [2] *essentially/goodly/well* recognized. The idea may seem peculiar to some people, but [3] *surprisingly/shockingly/unpredictably* there is clear evidence of the partnership. Take the example of dolphins, which are [4] *wildly/widely/hardly* known for their healing qualities. Dogs have also been used to detect cancer cells very [5] *deeply/professionally/accurately* in patients and are [6] *often/rarely/hardly* even taken around hospital wards to be introduced to [7] *seriously/hugely/deadly* ill patients. The effects of this particular partnership are [8] *importantly/really/well* documented and have led to animals being used [9] *frequently/seldom/lots* to supplement conventional medicine. [10] *Evident/Clearly/Oddly*, the conclusion is to make more money available for research into how animals can benefit humans.

3 Which pattern does the paragraph in 2 follow? Which **organizing words** are used to emphasize each element of the pattern?

a   situation – examples – effects – conclusion
b   situation – effects – reasons – examples – conclusion

4 Complete sentences a–i with **an organizing word** from the box.

> idea   information   issue   knowledge   measure
> opinion   problem   scheme   solution

a   The best way to improve public health is to provide people with all the facts, but the .... needs to be made simple.
b   It is often suggested that national health systems should be modernized. However, many people are opposed to the .... of modernization.
c   Our programme to introduce new equipment succeeded in reducing waiting lists, but the improvement .... met with considerable resistance.
d   The government should invest more money in preventing drug abuse. This .... , if taken, would save many lives.
e   Obesity is on the rise in many countries and not just in the developed world. It is now an .... that demands immediate attention.
f   More nurses need to be trained rather than doctors. This, I feel, is the best .... to the current crisis.
g   People are often aware of the dangers of smoking, but even with this widespread .... , it is difficult to persuade them to stop.
h   Some people are against the involvement of private companies in health care, but this .... is held by fewer people nowadays.
i   Lack of health care is making the lives of many people miserable, yet it is a .... that can be easily tackled.

5 For each of a–h, read the first sentence, then complete the follow-up sentence with your own ideas. Use the **organizing words** in italics to help you.

a   Some people are concerned that increasing numbers of old people will mean more spending on health care.

This *issue* ....

b   Conventional and alternative medicine can complement each other.

This *idea* could ....

c   In the future, health care will be much cheaper and for everyone.

This *prediction* ....

d   The pace of change within many national health systems is speeding up.

Initially, this may be a *problem*, but ....

e   Health care costs are now worrying planners throughout the world.

The *situation*, however, ...

f   More emphasis should be put on preventive medicine, like health education.

Measures like this ....

g   Acupuncture is becoming more and more popular around the world.

Not surprisingly, it is a *trend* ....

h   If people live longer, then this can lead to other costs and problems.

This is a *matter* that ....

6 Choose one of the topics a–c below. Make a list of ideas for the topic you have chosen. Use the **organizing words** in the box to trigger ideas.

a   the connection between music and health

b   how alternative therapies can influence health

c   the connection between exercise and health

> conclusion   effect   idea   information   issue   knowledge
> matter   measure   opinion   prediction   problem
> scheme   solution   trend   view   example

Technique

Aim to use at least one organizing word in each paragraph you write.

7 Write your own paragraph based on your ideas in 6. To plan your answer, ask yourself these questions.

a   What paragraph organization can I use?

b   Which connecting words can I use to link the pattern I have chosen to write?

c   Which examples can I use to justify my ideas in each paragraph?

Verb-subject agreement

8 Complete the following sentences with *is, are, has,* or *have*.

a The number of people who are suffering from stress .... on the increase.

b The fact that people live longer nowadays .... led to an increased number of elderly people in society.

c Predictions about how long a patient with cancer will live .... often inaccurate.

d A ban on advertising all types of junk food .... probably the only way to stop the spread of obesity.

e The pressurized situation in many hospitals .... resulted in a stressed workforce and low morale amongst nurses.

f Elderly people who have a large family .... generally healthier and happier than those who have fewer contacts with other people.

g The reason why allergies are becoming more common .... still not known.

h An increasing number of patients seem to be dissatisfied with conventional medicine and .... turned to alternative therapies.

9 In sentences a–g, replace the countable nouns in italics with an uncountable noun from the box. Make any other necessary changes in verb forms or pronouns.

> progress   evidence   information   work
> advice   research   equipment

Technique

Make sure you check that the subjects and the verbs in your sentences agree.

a Everyone is aware today of the bad effects of smoking on people's health. These *facts* are published all around us, even on cigarette packets.

....

b Most doctors recommend a diet low in sugar and fat, and high in fibre. Unfortunately, these *suggestions* are not often followed.

....

c Many nurses nowadays do not carry out basic care such as washing and feeding patients. Instead, these *tasks* are carried out by health care assistants.

....

d Enormous *advances* have been made in understanding how disease spreads, but the possibility of a worldwide pandemic is still with us.

....

e Many people enjoy keeping fit in the gym by using rowing machines, walking machines, and so on. However, these *devices* can be dangerous if they are not used properly.

....

f Many doctors do not believe in homeopathic medicine. However, there are certainly some *indications* that it is more than just a placebo.

....

g Some *studies* have been carried out which show that elderly people live longer if they live with a partner.

....

Practice Test 9

Task 1

You should spend about 20 minutes on this task.

The graph below shows the average monthly use of a health club in Miami, Florida by all full-time members over last year. The pie charts show the age profile of male and female members.

Summarize the information by selecting and reporting the main features, and make comparisons where relevant.

Write at least 150 words.

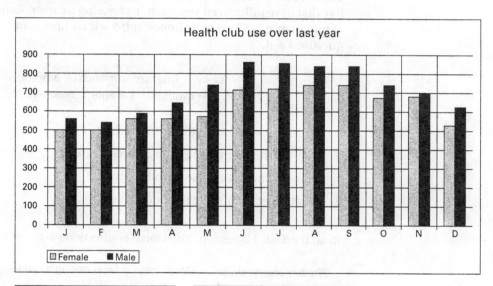

Health club use over last year

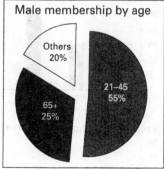

Male membership by age

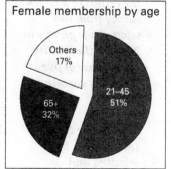

Female membership by age

Task 2

You should spend about 40 minutes on this task.
Write about the following topic:

The number of elderly people in the world is increasing. What do you think are the positive and negative effects of this trend?

Give reasons for your answer and include any relevant examples from your own knowledge or experience.
Write at least 250 words.

Individual and society

Unit aims

Task 1	Task 2
Word order	Paragraph structure
Linking using *with*	Task 2 revision
Task 1 revision	Relevant and irrelevant information

Task 1 **Word order**

1 The list below contains factors which influence career choice. Choose the five that have influenced you most in choosing a career. Rank them in order of importance 1–5 (1 = most important; 5 = least important). Then answer questions a–d.

> money   interest   friends   ambition
> role models   parents   teachers

a   Why have you chosen these five factors?

b   How did they contribute to your career choice?

c   Why did you not choose the other factors?

d   What other factors might influence you?

2 Read the Task 1 question. Then answer questions a–e.

The bar charts show the results of a Greek survey from two selected age groups in 2003 on the relative importance of five factors in choosing a career.

Summarize the information by selecting and reporting the main features, and make comparisons where relevant.

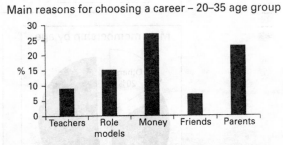

Main reasons for choosing a career – 20–35 age group

Main reasons for choosing a career – 40–50 age group

a   What does each chart refer to generally? Look at the captions.

b   What do the items along the bottom of the bar charts refer to?

c   How do the bar charts relate to each other?

d   What are the most noticeable features of the first bar chart?

e   What are the most noticeable features of the second bar chart?

3 Reorder the words in italics in the model text below.

Model text

The bar charts provide information from a Greek survey about [1] *reasons/the/for/main/career/a/choosing* among two age groups, 20–35 and 40–50.

It is clear that the two groups [2] *the/influenced/were/various/by/factors* to different degrees, with the most influential factors which contributed to career choice for the 20–25 age group being money (approximately 27 per cent) and then parents (23 per cent). However, the factors [3] *the/age/were/for/reverse/group/the/40–50*, with parents affecting them most at 30 per cent.

[4] *teachers/as/regards/role/and/models*, the relative importance of each was again the other way round: [5] *nine/fifteen/and/respectively/group/per/cent/for/younger/the*, and fourteen and eleven per cent for the older.

[6] *similarity/only/the/the/two/groups/between/age* was that friends had less influence over career choice for the younger and older groups [7] *factors/than/any/other*, seven and ten per cent respectively.

4 Six of the sentences a–h contain a word in the wrong place. Correct each sentence by moving the word to the right place.

Example

Traveller numbers have decreased over period in the question.
Traveller numbers have decreased over *the* period in question.

a   The specialist sales of tours have fallen recently.

b   In 2006, more males than females took up individual sports rather than team activities.

c   As can be seen, more people from the younger age group travel on their own, in sharp contrast to those over sixty.

d   It is clear that the number of flats by single people in occupied major cities in the West is putting pressure on housing.

e   From the graphs, it can be concluded that are young people much more mobile than previous generations.

f   The noticeable pursuit of a professional career among both men and women has led to a reduction in the birth rate.

g   There are similarities in the presentation of the several data.

h   Overall, the chart shows that the media people are responsible for turning into celebrities.

Task 2 Paragraph structure

1 For each Task 2 question below, put the sentences that follow in the most logical order to create a paragraph.

> *1 Ambition is a negative attribute of a person's character. Do you agree or disagree with this statement?*

a This is because, even when they realize an ambition, they are still not satisfied.
b It is certainly true that ambitious people do not always create happiness for themselves or others.
c If we look at the businessman who wants to earn a six-figure salary, we see that in most cases, when he reaches this position, he will still want more power or an even higher salary.

> *2 Particular cultures are under threat nowadays due to the fact that we are living in a global village. What do you think can be done to protect a society's traditional values and culture?*

a Nor does it mean that they will fail to respect and value other people's cultures.
b One way to protect traditional values and customs is simply to teach people to value their own culture.
c On the contrary, it will give them the confidence to operate in our global village without feeling that their own identity is under threat.
d This does not mean that they have to resist the current movement towards greater international trade.

> *3 Emails are the most valuable tool for communication in the twenty-first century. To what extent do you agree or disagree?*

a They can exchange ideas and discuss things more often as they are working, and the result may be a better end product.
b This allows people to work together on the same project even if they are on opposite sides of the world.
c Emails have certainly had far-reaching effects on people's ability to communicate.
d It is now possible for people to correspond cheaply and at length from anywhere as long as they have a connection.

2 Match each of the paragraphs above 1–3 with the correct structure below a–c.

a general statement – reason why this statement is true – example
b general statement – reason why this statement is true – effect – second effect
c statement of what should happen – statement that a negative result will not occur – statement that a second negative result will not occur – positive result

3 Read the following two essay questions. For each question, choose one of the paragraph structures in 2 on page 81 and write a paragraph which could form part of an answer, following the structure you have chosen.

> *Money does not make happiness. To what extent do you agree or disagree?*

> *It is better to reform criminals instead of just punishing them. What measures could be taken to attempt to integrate law-breakers back into society?*

Relevant and irrelevant information

4 The three paragraphs below relate to the Task 1 questions in 1 on page 81. In each paragraph, there are several options. Choose the options which are most relevant to the question.

Text 1

1 Another reason why ambition is not always good is that ambitious people may use unfair or dishonest means of reaching their goal. For example, they may

  a work so hard that they neglect their families.
  b take the credit for work that they have not done.

2 In some cases, they may damage the careers of people who they see as rivals, perhaps by

  a making false accusations about them to their employers.
  b stealing their money and possessions.

3 In the most extreme cases, they may turn to serious crime. .... provides a clear example of this.

  a Shakespeare's story of Macbeth
  b The story of Sinbad the sailor

Text 2

4 One way to ensure that people value their traditional culture is to focus on language. With the global dominance of English, some minority languages such as .... may feel under threat.

  a Welsh or Estonian
  b Chinese or Arabic

5 If people are made familiar with the history and literature of their own language, then

  a they will be more able to talk to older people about it.
  b they will appreciate their own culture more.

6 This could be done by arranging arts festivals or writing competitions. For example, in the UK

  a there are many prizes which novelists and poets can win.
  b there is an annual festival to celebrate the best of Welsh writing and culture.

Text 3

7 However, the effects of the Internet on communication are not all positive. Emails can be written and replied to very quickly which means that

a people often do not consider carefully what they have written.
b people can check their inbox two or three times a day.

8 Another problem is that people simply send and receive too many emails. .... The result of this is that they spend time dealing with this constant stream of messages instead of doing their real work.

a Children, for example, love to contact their friends frequently by email.
b An office worker, for example, may receive twenty or thirty emails a day.

5 Read the Task 2 question. Then answer questions a–c below.

> *The current interest in famous people's private lives has negative effects both for those people and for society as a whole. Newspapers should not be allowed to publish details of people's private lives unless it is clearly in the public interest.*
>
> *To what extent do you agree or disagree?*

a Think of a famous person who has been in the news recently for something unconnected with his/her job. What were the effects of this?
b How relevant is your example to the question. If possible, compare your example with a partner. Which is the most relevant to the question?
c Write a general statement–example paragraph, using the example you have chosen.

Task 2 revision

6 Read the Task 2 techniques in the questionnaire. Decide how often you do these things.

Task 2 techniques questionnaire

Tick the appropriate box.

	Always	Sometimes	Never
I match the organization of my essay to the question.	☐	☐	☐
I use the paragraph structure.	☐	☐	☐
I divide my essay into paragraphs.	☐	☐	☐
I use **organizing words** to help develop my sentences.	☐	☐	☐
I use a range of **linking phrases** – *like, because, for example* – to trigger my ideas.	☐	☐	☐
I write a short introduction which paraphrases the question.	☐	☐	☐
I know that I must write at least 250 words.	☐	☐	☐
I leave myself time to check my answer.	☐	☐	☐
I develop functions like *advantages, disadvantages, solutions, measures, causes* by using *reasons, examples, results, effects*.	☐	☐	☐
I can state my opinion clearly and contradict other opinions.	☐	☐	☐

7 Which phrases can you use as **trigger words** for each of the following **functions**? Make your own list.

a Example: *For example,* ....

b Reason: *because* ....

c Effect: *As a result,* ....

d Additional information: *Moreover,* ....

e Hypothesis: *If* ....

f Contrast: *but* ....

g Concession: *Although* ....

h Conclusion: *And so* ....

8 Some functions are related so that one suggests the other. Complete the list below with related functions. Are the combinations fixed or can you combine them in any way?

a Problem and ....

b Measures and ....

c Cause and ....

d Reason and ....

e Example and ....

f Effect and ....

g Additional information and ....

h Condition/Hypothesis and ....

i Concession and ....

9 Read the Task 2 question below, then use the **trigger words** to develop sentences a–f with your own ideas.

> *Too much emphasis is put on earning money rather than looking for a good quality of life. To what extent do you agree with this idea?*

a Money is not as important as friends, because ....
   ....

b For many people, keeping fit and healthy is the main factor which is necessary for a good quality of life. However, ...
   ....

c If one is content with life, then ....
   ....

d What is involved in achieving a good quality of life depends on many factors rather than just one. For example, ...
   ....

e Happiness and contentment are more important than the pursuit of freedom. The latter aim ....
   ....

f Many people living in poor housing conditions are still happy. So the idea that ....
   ....

10 Write your own paragraph about the importance of family in maintaining a good quality of life. Write about 60–80 words.

Practice Test 10

Task 1

You should spend about 20 minutes on this task.

The bar chart below shows the percentage of people in Great Britain living alone by age and sex in 2004/2005.

Summarize the information by selecting and reporting the main features, and make comparisons where relevant.

Write at least 150 words.

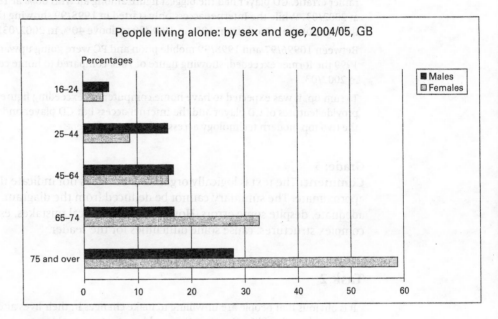

Task 2

You should spend about 40 minutes on this task.
Write about the following topic:

Individuals can do nothing to change society. Any new developments can only be brought about by governments and large institutions. How far do you agree or disagree?

Give reasons for your answer and include any relevant examples from your own knowledge or experience.
Write at least 250 words.

Sample answers

The publishers stress that these are not official grades and are for guidance only. There is no guarantee that these answers would obtain these grades in the test.

Task 1

> The graph indicates the variation of the private use of Internet, PC, mobile phones and CD player in the UK from 1996 to 2003.
>
> The trend in four elements of the study was upward except in mobile phone that was rather erratic. CD player had the biggest figure among all with 60% at 1996/97 and 80% at 2002/03. While the Internet access only started in 1998/99 showing the lowest figure throughout the period (from 10% in 1998/99 to above 40% in 2002/03).
>
> Between 10996/97 and 1998/99 mobile phon and PC were going upward while just after 1999 the former exceeded, showing figure of 70% compared to home computers with 55% in 2002/03.
>
> To sum up, it was expected to have home computers as exceeding figure in the study as they provide features of CD player and the Internet access but CD player and mobile phon were the two top modern technology access in homes. *(154 words)*

Grade: 5

Comment: The text is logically organized, but does not indicate that figures are approximate. The summary cannot be deduced from the diagram. Vocabulary is adequate, despite some errors. However, grammatical mistakes, especially faulty complex structures, cause some difficulties for the reader.

Task 2

> It is obvious that people are unwilling to make changes in their lives after being accustomed to a certain style of life. However this could cause many problems.
>
> Take for example, people who leave their country and going abroad. They might face many issues. First of all, they have to adapt to a new culture and habit which might be completely different from their native country. Moreover, it takes time to adapt to weather and to the style of new life wich may be different from where they lived before.
>
> There is another changes in life. For example, some people at a certain moment in their live have to change their career, regardless of the reasons. It is quite difficult they find not easy to acquire experience in their new job and difficult to make new friends at work.
>
> In my opinion, people should be flexible. For people who leaving their country to live and work in another country I agree that they might have many problems such as a new culture and language and habits but the integration with people it could solve the problem. By the time, they will find themselves a part of the new society. People who change their career the only thing to do it is to concentrate in their new job. Experience that they need they will acquire with time.
>
> In conclusion, people have to ready for any changes in their lives as no guarantee for anyone that the life will be stable forever. *(250 words)*

Grade: 6

Comments: All parts of the prompt are covered, but the content is somewhat repetitive. Organization and paragraphing is satisfactory, with some effective use of links. Vocabulary is generally adequate. However, complex sentences are usually faulty and there are many grammatical errors.

Practice Test 2

Task 1

The graph shows the contribution of different sectors to the UK economy in the 20th century. In particular it compares the agricultural, manufacturing and business and financial sectors.

Firstly, agriculture sector shows the higher value at the beginning of the period (around 50% in the first 50 years of the century). By the 1975, it had suffered a dramatic decrease (15%) followed by a drop to almost zero in 2000. By contrast, business and finantial sector were almost zero at the beginning but it sharply increased during the period.

Manufacturing sector seems to follow the trend of agriculture, starting with a value of 45% in 1900. In 1950 it began to fall till 1975 where it was below 35%. At the end of the period the percentage for manufacturing reaches 20%.

In general, agricultural and manufacturing sector has a similar trends but the former dropped much more at the end of the century than the latter. In contrast, the trend of business and financial increased during the period. *(168 words)*

Grade: 6
Comments: Use of the rubric unchanged reduces the word count. The information is logically ordered, but the business sector data is omitted. Vocabulary is adequate and usually appropriate, as is the range of sentence forms, but there are some important errors.

Task 2

Studying the history is one of the most important subjects in the circulum of primary and secondary schools. Some people argue that there is no benefit of that and history can be substituted by other more important subjects. However, it is not a logical opinion for many reasons.

Although it is true that the events that are studied in history happened in the past, it is also true that it represent a valuable human experience. This can be very useful in planning for the future. If humans know the mistakes that had been done and caused disastriase events in the past, they will try to avoid doing the same mistakes in the future.

Moreover studying the past of other nations will give the opportunity to know more about their society. This will help in building good relationships between different countries.

Children are the people who will lead the world in the future so they should prepare for this role. The knowledge which can be gained from the history is one of the most important sources for their skills of understanding the human society. As much as they learn from the history, they will be efficient in their ability to decide when they face any problem in the future. Also the history can give a good information about the development in different branches of science. Some of these information may have a good value for inventors.

In conclusion, it is undeniable that history, the summary of human experience, is very important in improvement of human's future if they can use it properly. *(261)*

Grade: 6
Comments: The topic is adequately covered, though there is some repetition. The order and paragraphing of ideas is mostly logical. Vocabulary is adequate and has some precision. Complex sentences are well managed, but there are many minor grammatical errors.

Practice Test 3

Task 1

The diagram illustrates the various stages in the desalination of seawater to make it suitable for drinking.

First of all, water is taken from the sea and then passed through a pre-treatment filter where the big impurities are removed. This backwash is then piped back into the sea through another filter. At the next stage in the process, the remaining water is forced through a membrane at high pressure and any impurities including salt are removed. After that, the seawater concentrate is returned to the sea while the remaining water goes through a post treatment process. In this phase, the water is treated with lime, chlorine and fluoride to make it drinkable before it is stored in a reservoir. Finally, the desalinated water is distributed to the integrated water supply system for people to use as drinking water.

Desalination involves a process of purification of water followed by filtration and adding chemical agents. *(153 words)*

Grade: 7

Comments: Interest is maintained by the flexible use of input language, and a wide range of vocabulary and skilfully deployed grammatical structures. All stages are covered accurately, though some additions are made. The overview should more logically be the second sentence.

Task 2

Great changes have taken place in our life along with development of society. As far as I am concerned, the Internet plays a big part in this.

First of all, with the opportunity of surfing internet or playing computer and video games, people have a more sedentary life style. Children no longer play games outside and get exercise but they spend time on the computer. This has bad effect on their health and can cause problems such as obesity.

Another problem is the negative effect on their relationship with their family. Internet access fills most young people's time, and even their leisure time, so this is the cause of their disconnection with their family and ultimately can have an effect on their social behaviour. A third problem is that not all internet sites are useful. Information is often not accurate and some sites are not suitable for children. Some internet sites like chat rooms can even be dangerous because you do not know who is the other person.

As regarding children's use of the Internet, the first solution must be with the parents.

They need to limit hours that children spend on the computer and to encourage them to have other hobbies and pastimes. There is an important need for them to spend more time to speak with their family than an electronic connection. Parents should also encourage children to use other means of information in addition to internet.

To conclude, I would say that the internet has brought many benefits and it will not disappear, therefore it is very important that we learnt to use it well so that we can reap the benefits and not the disadvantages. *(278 words)*

Grade: 7

Comments: The topic is considered fully, with ideas presented in a clear progression with mostly logical paragraphing. A good range of vocabulary gives flexibility and precision to the writing. Sentence structure is reasonably varied, but minor grammatical errors are frequent.

Practice Test 4

Task 1

The bar chart shows the figures for qualifications attained in women and men in Wales in 2001 and 2002 in percentages.

The information can be divided into three groups. The first category includes degree and higher education qualification. The percentages were around 13% and approximately 11% for men and women respectively for degree but for higher education qualification 8% for male and 9% for female.

For GCE A level and GCSE grade A to C the percentage was much higher compared with the other two groups. The number of males in GCE A level was roughly 28% but for females about 15%. However, the GCSE grade A–C showed a reverse pattern, 18% and 28% for men and women respectively.

The figures for the third group were much lower. Other qualifications figures cited 12% for men and 11% for women. No qualifications were recorded for higher numbers of men and women, 20% and 23%.

Overall, men had more higher degrees whereas women had more GCE or equivalent qualifications. *(168 words)*

Grade: 6

Comments: Details are accurately listed, but there is no real overview. The key points are not brought out. However, the vocabulary shows some variety and precision. Despite minor errors of grammar, simple sentences are used well, but complex structures are lacking.

Task 2

To some extent I disagree with the notion that competitive sports cannot be part of the school curriculum. However, the amount of time given should not be overlooked.

Sports as a whole is an important part of growing up. Students regardless of their age take part in exercise individually or as a team member. Take primary schools for instance, they have playgrounds and fairly enough facilities from which students can take benefit.

In secondary schools students' attitude to sport changes. The demand for more facilities and equipments rises. As can be seen, more and more teenagers turn to football, swimming, even body building outside school hours. They try to make use of the facilities available to them at school as well. What is important is time which should not be spent on taken up sport and not doing other school work or study.

On the other hand, considering the availability of the facilities to all schools is not a bad idea. To illustrate this, some schools are well equipped while others do poorly. No matter how little the facility students should be encouraged to take part in competitive sports.

All in all, I think sport was part of everyday life in the past and is in today's sport attracting societies. The best place you start your life after home is school. Everyone decides what to do at early age. As for sport, it was part of curriculum vitae in the past and will be in the future of course, with a better time management. *(254 words)*

Grade: 6

Comments: Though the ideas are relevant and sufficient, faults in ordering and use of links sometimes cause difficulty for the reader. A good range of vocabulary is mostly used with precision. A limited but accurate range of complex sentences are deployed.

Task 1

Between 1990 and 2005 there were so many changes that took place in town of Templeton in term of developments.

On the west of the river that divide the city into two parts, there main buildings were constructed replacing part of the green area and the suburban home. Besides, more houses were built to reduce the green area furthermore. To the south of the above developments, all houses were demolished and new buildings raised up instead together with supermarket.

To the east of the river, an airport was built in an area previously covered by trees and more houses were added to the area around the hospital.

A major development took place in south east art of city where a factory was constructed and ferry service was established, replacing all of the old houses and the tree forest that occupied the area before. Moreover, a new railway track was laid down alongside the embankment. *(155 words)*

Grade: 6

Comments: All key points were highlighted, but lacked a clear overview. The data was logically and coherently arranged. The vocabulary was adequate for the task, but included some inappropriacies. Sentence structures were varied and usually well controlled, despite frequent grammatical errors.

Task 2

Many people thinks that the world existing problems are only matter the young generation as they are the candidate who are facing them now and in the future.

Although a considerable percentage of the public might refer to these hazards as hazards for the young predominantly, yet many of these concerns are actually brought into the scene by the old people. The previous generation are those who lived the new developments in science and technology that brought with them pollution, poverty and part of it also possible distinction of many species of plants and animals.

So they raise the alarms for those radical and serious consequences. It is often suggested that old generation are passing by and not interested in what happening and only the young who gives those alerts considerable thoughts.

However from what we are experiencing now, that many of green people are old and work actively to preserve animal rights and fight fiercely against global warming and environmental pollution. This give us that the present world concerns are a shared interest of both old and new generations. Although many activist on these issues appears in the media and they are from the youth, still and probably equal number from the old follow the same routes.

Actually no one in this life want to destroy our planet. Definitely every parent is of concern about his offspring lives thereafter, and selfishness does not dominate our thinking at all. What one should be aware of is that such threats are not always discussed or contemplated in the right way by old or young generation. *(264 words)*

Grade: 5

Comments: Though the ideas are relevant and well argued, cohesion is faulty and the paragraphing is not logical. Vocabulary is fairly varied and precise. However, complex structures, though frequent, are always faulty, with grammatical errors causing some strain for the reader.

Practice Test 6

Task 1

The table illustrates the percentages of both young boys and girls who listened to music in the previous month in the capital of Japan.

The most striking feature is that males were more interested in music than their female counterparts except for listening to CDs (19% and 22% respectively). The highest rate was 79% for boys who were interested in MP3-players, while with regard to the same type of players for girls the proportion was 40% which was almost similar to the percentage of the Internet (42%). With respect to live music, females recorded 44%.

Turning to the pie chart, 70% of young Japanese people prefer live music, whereas recorded music rate was 26% and those who answered Don't know their rate was just 4%.

In conclusion, young females spent less time listening to favourite music compared to the opposite sex. Regarding preference of music Live music scored the top percentage. *(150 words)*

Grade: 6

Comments: The key points are mainly covered, but there is an important error (paragraph 3). It could be ordered more logically. However, cohesive devices are well used. Vocabulary is adequate for the purpose. There are a variety of sentence structures, but their complexity sometimes causes difficulty for the reader.

Task 2

There is no doubt that the number of visitors and businessmen and women who are travelling abroad has been increasing markedly in recent years. However, not surprisingly, understanding the culture of local people brings many benefits to all types of visitors as well as problems for those who do not understand a new culture.

First of all, no sensible person can deny the importance of breaking down barriers between countries. By this I mean, people from different lands can socialize effectively and relate emotionally regardless of their race and religion, if they take time to learn languages and to find out about where they are going before they travel. As a result, the tension between people from different backgrounds would be melted.

Another important advantage that needs to be taken into account is that travellers can broaden their horizons by travelling. In other words, people who travel for business or tourism definitely would gain a lot of information from their host society. Knowing how to behave can help businessmen make lots of money for themselves and for their companies. Undoubtedly business and tourism play a pivotal role in employing of people and reviving the local economy in their own countries and when they travel.

On the other hand lack of understanding of the culture and traditions of people may lead to misunderstanding and even increased tension between different communities, simply because the background of any society can act as a mirror to reflect the nature personality and behaviour of people. Certainly, when we know these vital things we can overcome many difficulties. *(262 words)*

Grade: 8

Comments: There are many ideas, well organized into paragraphs and highlighted clearly, despite minor lapses in focus. The wide range of vocabulary exhibits flexibility and precision, with only occasional inappropriacies. A variety of sentence structures are used, containing no significant errors.

Task 1

The two bar chart illustrate the percentage of purchase on-line tickets of concert, cinema, and theatre in (Australia, the UK, and Malaysia), by a selected age group and how the interest was accessed over the first three months of 2006.

Purchases for the age group 25–44 was the same in the western countries at 55%, whereas in Malaysia, it was just under 40%. Surprisingly, the percentage was very close in the UK and Malaysia around 40% for the age group 65+, with a slight increase in Australia to about 45%.

In terms of the most common means of access to buy tickets, the chart shows that the desktop computers was the predominant means in Malaysia the UK and Australia at about 60%, 62% and 68% respectively. Next came the laptop, with a close percentage in Australia and Malaysia around (45% each), while there was a moderate drop to 30.5% in the UK.

The data might give us an indication about the online purchasing. *(163 words)*

Grade: 5

Comments: Excessive use of the rubric reduces the word count and incurs a penalty. There are many inaccuracies in the data, which lacks an overview. Vocabulary and links are inaccurately used, but grammar and sentence structures are adequate for the task.

Task 2

The question of whether money could be more usefully applied to tackle the crisis around the world rather than spent it on space research is a very controversial issue and it is now a matter of considerable public concern. There are, therefore, people on both sides of the argument who have feelings either for or against.

Many people believe that money should be spent to solve food crisis in Africa and South Asia. Drought, for example, left Africa with famine. Every 30 seconds an African child dies of hunger and about 45% of children in South Asia suffer from malnutrition. Similarly, the global issue is the conflict of AIDS in Africa. Although, there are numerous factors in the spread of HIV/AIDS , it is largely recognized as a disease of poverty. Medicines, for instance, are very expensive and the government in poor countries can not afford to treat the disease, therefore millions are dying, while in rich countries people are living longer.

Having said that, however, some people oppose the former argument. They claim that space research has brought enormous benefits to mankind. Recently, NASA has launched Satellites for weather and climate, which will give the scientists a unique view of earth's atmosphere, helping them to improve their abilities to forecast weather and predict climate change.

From what has been discussed above we may draw the conclusion that both points of view have their merits. Although, human life has priority in our societies, advanced research should be carried out to find another source of energy, water on other planet, and to understand the planets and its' effect on earth for the benefit of all. *(276 words)*

Grade: 7

Comments: Though there are sufficient ideas and evidence, the first paragraph adds nothing. Ideas are logically organized and paragraphed, but the conclusion is not clearly articulated. There is a good range of vocabulary and sentence structures, despite some jarring punctuation errors.

Practice Test 8

Task 1

The table illustrates expected cost of the three environmental projects in three different parts of the world in the next five years.

The estimated cost of the African project in Year 1 is 10.5 million dollars, almost half of the projected cost for Central America (20 million) and about one third of the Asian project (30 million). It is predicted that West Africa will spend less money in the following years than in Year 1, falling to 3.5 million in Year 5. Central America shows a similar pattern. In Year 5 expected cost of project is 5 million dollars which is four times less than in year 1. However, in South East Asia in year 5 spending will rise to 50 million dollars.

Regarding the pie chart, 50% of projected cost will cover salaries. The rest 50% will be shared on training and office expenses, 10% each, while 30% is expected set up costs.

To sum up South East Asia has the highest projected cost for environmental projects for the next five years. *(173 words)*

Grade: 7

Comments: The key points are presented logically and are suitably highlighted by cohesive devices. However, the overview could be more fully developed. The vocabulary range allows some flexibility of presentation. Sentence structures are varied, but some basic grammatical errors occur.

Task 2

Many people are moving out of big cities into the countryside to live to escape from city problems. This is causing problems because most the jobs that are available are in the cities so people have to travel back into the cities again to work. The transport system cannot cope so people are using their own cars and the countryside is affected by the traffic jams.

One solution to encourage people to stay in cities is to improve the quality of life there. More money could be spent reducing crime, as this is one of the main reasons why people leave cities. For example, more policemen can be employed for city centres, which happened in New York and is happening here in UK. As well as safe places to work and live city centres could be made more friendly and welcoming. The environment can be made cleaners and more agreeable to live and work in. This way people might be encouraged to stay rather than moving out.

A very different way to tackle the problem would to move some of the jobs out of city to smaller cities or towns. People could then still live in the countryside and enjoy it and only have to travel short distances to work. Another step is to encourage workers to spend part of their working week at home, perhaps two days and then to go into work in the other days. This is happening more and more in many parts of the world.

There are other ways to overcome the situation but these are the most important. *(264 words)*

Grade: 7

Comments: The writer's proposals are clearly presented, with logical paragraphing, but the conclusion could be more fully developed. The progression of ideas is well marked. The vocabulary is very appropriate to the task. Sentence structures are reasonably varied, without significant errors.

Task 1

The graph gives information about the average monthly use of a Health Club in Miami Florida by full time members last year.

One of the most striking features of the graph is that use the gym was higher in summer compared to the other months of the year. In January 550 males visited the gym the figure decreased slightly. After that there was a significant increase in the number of males membership from January to June. In June the figure hit the highest point of 8500 but in July there was a slight reduction to December. The trend for females membership follow the same. However from July to September 7200 females used the gym in every month.

Turning to pie chart, 4% more of male membership aged between 21 and 45 used the facilities in gym compared to females. Thirty-two percent of female member had age 65+ in contrast to 25% of males. Twenty percent of other age group among males had the membership compared to 17% of females.

Overall, higher number of males used the gym than women. *(179 words)*

Grade: 5
Comments: Copying the rubric reduces the word count. Data is listed mechanically and, and includes serious errors. The selection, which is not wholly logical, lacks an overview. The range of both vocabulary and sentence structures is limited, with many grammatical errors.

Task 2

There is no doubt that age expectancy has increased over the last twenty years. The question of whether the increasing number of elderly people causes positive effects or negative is a matter of dispute. As far as I am concerned it has negative effect for a number of reasons.

Some people are of the opinion that this trend should be increased because there might be more experienced workers in society. People will work longer than now. This might have a possitive effect on economy. As we know, these people give tax to the government. Moreover if we ask anyone, they are happy to live longer as they devote most of their lives to working. In retirement age elderly people need comfort and such people desire to do many things that they did not do before. Thus, increasing aged population gives hope to the seniors who would like to enjoy their lives.

However, I do believe that higher aged population needs higher investment as people in elder age suffer from diseases such as heart disease, stroke, diabetis, Alzehamer disease. Governments need to invest a colosal sums of money treating such patients. Further more people in elder age become more dependent to others as these people nee to be supervised by other people. I think nobody likes to live with other people and use the facilities that are not belong to them. Therefore seniors suffer from depression and psychological problems. At the same time if people work longer, there is not promotion for the younger generation because most positions are occupied by the elderly people.

To conclude, I feel that the negative effects on society outweigh the positive effects because of the above reasons. *(282 words)*

Grade: 6
Comments: There are plenty of ideas, but paragraphing is not well managed. However, the sentences tend to be clearly linked. The range of vocabulary is adequate for the purpose, as is the variety of sentence structures, but grammatical errors are obtrusive.

Practice Test 10

Task 1

The bar chart illustrates the percentage of people in Great Britain living alone according to their age and gender from 2004 to 2005.

It is immediately apparent that living alone increased as people were getting older and the percentage of females outnumbered the opposite sex. For instance, the last category of age showed that the overwhelming majority of people living alone was females about 59% compared only to 28% of males.

As regards males living on their own we can see a little difference in the second third and fourth groups of age. They almost had the similar percentage. However this was not the case in the first category which was just 5%. Unlike men, women's predominance began in the 65/74 year olds which showed a dramatic change. For example the percentage of females was 32% as opposed to 15% for males. Prior to this group, the third category of age had almost the same percentage.

By and large, living alone was common among women as they go older. The 35–44 year olds was the only category with a noticeable male predominance. *(182 words)*

Grade: 6

Comments: The rubric is copied, reducing the word count. There is a clear overview, with well highlighted main points. However, organization is less clear in the third paragraph. Vocabulary and grammar are fairly varied, but there are various inaccurate usages.

Task 2

There is little doubt that governments and large institutions implement many innovations into our society. However, from my point of view, they are only able to do so with the help of ideas from individual citizens.

For a start, every part of society, including government and large institutions, consists of individual members. Governments have the rights to the further use of the new ideas and in fact should always listen to them. For example, a Ukrainian engineer called Platon introduced the idea of building a bridge across the river in Kiev. Seeing the strategic importance of this bridge the government provided funds to build it. And now the whole of society benefits from the use of one man's idea.

Furthermore in London, the Mayor, Mr Livingstone, announced a competition which can be entered by individuals to find a new way to provide air conditioning for the underground system. This is yet another example of how governments and large institutions rely on the creativity of individuals to be inventive and bring about change.

Some people might say that governments have the strength, power and money to realise and introduce new ideas on their own. In the case of institutions they possess up to date equipment and massive facilities. However I would say that they are not enough to allow them to contribute to society as a whole. This is where creativity and outstanding ideas come in. So if an individual's efforts are combined with the governments' s power and money, there would be many changes that could benefit everyone.

In conclusion, both individuals and large organizations, including governments need to work in partnership to bring about any beneficial change. *(278 words)*

Grade: 8

Comments: The writer does not fully address the topic but does present a clear and logically sequenced argument, supported by evidence. Cohesive devices are used effectively. The range of vocabulary produces fluency and precision. Sentence structure is varied and grammatically accurate.

Key

Unit 1

1

Possible answer

Students' own answers. Graphs associated with iPod and DVD may be expected to be rising (c or f), whereas graphs associated with audio and video cassettes may be expected to be falling (a, e, g, or h).

2

1 g   2 c   3 d   4 a   5 b
6 h   7 f   8 e   9 h   10 e

3

2   rose
3   fluctuated
4   fluctuated
5   dropped
6   fell, levelled off
7   rose, climbed
8   declined
9   decreased, levelled off
10 dropped

4

Slow: steadily, gradually, slightly
Fast: wildly, sharply, dramatically, suddenly

5

a   There were wild fluctuations in spice exports from Africa over the period.
b   There was a gradual fall in the development of new products.
c   Research investment has decreased noticeably.
d   There was a significant drop in the purchases of tickets last month.
e   There was a significant rise in the number of sites on the Internet.
f   The sale of mangos decreased suddenly.

g   The number of visitors at the theme park fluctuated very slightly.
h   Sugar imports declined gradually.
i   There has been a slow increase in the quality of food in supermarkets.
j   There was a remarkable fluctuation in the number of air travellers.

6

a   African spice exports
b   new product development
d   ticket purchases
e   Internet sites
f   mango sales
g   theme park visitors
i   supermarket food quality

7

b $85,000
c $125,000
d $120,000
e $130,000

8

a   months of the year
b   thousands of dollars
c   Sales went up for Internet Express, Wi-fi Cafe, and Cafe Cool, but down for The Tea Room.
d   Between different cafes and between different months for the same cafe.

9

2   noun   3   verb
4   noun   5   adverb
6   verb   7   verb

10

1 d   2 g   3 e   4 f   5 a
6 c   7 b

1

a   drawbacks
b   reasons
c   causes
d   solutions

2

b   disadvantages, agree or disagree
c   advantages/benefits, disadvantages
d   agree or disagree
e   advantages/benefits
f   causes, solutions
g   measures

3

b   three parts, two statements plus question
c   one part
d   two parts, statement plus question
e   two parts, statement plus question
f   three parts, statement plus two questions
g   two parts, statement plus question

4

Possible answers

Work: people have less stable jobs
Technology: continually developing new computer systems and electronic devices
Travel: air travel is still on the increase and becoming cheaper
Communication: people are using text messages more
Health: life expectancy is increasing

5

a   first sentence
b   causes, solutions

6

They are answering: can you suggest some possible solutions?
They suggest: encouraging employees to relax, providing gyms and massage therapy, training employees to manage their time better.
Results: people will be more efficient and productive; the workplace will be happier.

7

1 c   2 f   3 d   4 a
5 b   6 e

8

a People should be encouraged to exercise more.
b The number of working hours should be reduced.
c One possibility is for the government to provide each employee with their own computer.
d Parents could be persuaded to spend more time with their children.
e The number of cars coming into cities should/could be restricted
f A good idea is for the government to build more skyscrapers.

9

a obesity (or stress)
b stress
c technology
d lack of discipline
e traffic congestion
f overcrowding

10

Possible answers

b As a result, people would be obliged to manage their time more effectively.
c This would enable them to work from home and avoid stressful journeys into work.
d This would lead to better communication between family members.
e Consequently, there would be less traffic congestion and journey times would be reduced.
f By doing this, they would ensure that there were fewer people living in crowded or substandard accommodation.

11

addition: and, furthermore
condition: if
example: for instance, for example

purpose: in order to
reason: because, since
result: consequently, and so, therefore, as a result

12

reason: because
result: as a result, and so
example: for example
solution: the obvious answer is

13

Possible answers

A

If people migrate to cities, they become trapped in poor, overcrowded accommodation and so their health deteriorates and as a result their quality of life may be no better than before. A good idea would be to try to create new jobs in the countryside. By doing this, people would not feel the need to move into cities which are already overcrowded.

B

People spend too much time watching TV. For example, some children stay up late watching TV in their bedroom instead of getting a good night's sleep. Consequently, they arrive at school tired and unable to learn. If households just have one TV in the main living area, then it will be easier to control how many hours are spent in front of it. This will lead to better results at school.

C

The development of tourism often creates resentment among local people because tourists do not help the local economy. For example, they may stay in international hotels which make large profits outside the country. The obvious answer is to encourage tourists to use locally available accommodation. Furthermore, by doing this, they would learn more about the country they are visiting.

Unit 2

Task 1

1

a paper money, around eighth century AD
b ballpoint pen, patented 1938 (other dates are Fahrenheit's thermometer 1714, Durand's tin can 1810, and Hunt's safety pin 1849)
c Students' own answers.
d There are many other important historical inventions. They could include paper, the light bulb, radio and TV.

2

a The bicycle was ranked as most important by most males and females.
b More females than males ranked the bicycle, mobile phone, and radio as the most important.
c More males than females ranked the car, computer, Internet, and TV as the most important.

3

a than
b popular
c less
d The least popular
e More
f The most popular
g Fewer
h less important
i than
j less

4

Possible answers
Not as many females as males chose the car.
Not as many males as females chose the mobile phone.

5

a More males than females chose the car.

b More women than men selected the mobile phone.

c The Internet was chosen by more males than females.

d More females than males picked the radio.

e Fewer males than females picked the radio.

f The computer was chosen by fewer females than males.

g The bicycle was selected by fewer males than females.

6

a Slightly
b considerably
c Many
d Substantially
e significantly
f practically
g far
h much
i Nearly

7

a nearly, practically

b considerably, many, substantially, significantly, far, much

c slightly

8

Possible answers

a Far more males than females chose the car.

b Considerably more women than men selected the mobile phone.

c The Internet was chosen by significantly more males than females.

d Substantially more females than males picked the radio.

e Significantly fewer males than females picked the radio.

f The computer was chosen by slightly fewer females than males.

g The bicycle was selected by slightly fewer males than females.

9

Possible answers

a The bar chart probably provides information about the number of people in two different age groups who had various interests.

b numbers of people
c interests/societies
d age groups
e There is no time reference.

10

1 c 2 e 3 a 4 f
5 d 6 b

11

Ending could come first: 2, 3, 4, 5, 6

Noun phrase only: *in comparison with*, *compared with*

12

Correct options

1 However, By contrast
2 but, while
3 but, whereas
4 far, considerably
5 but, although
6 significantly, noticeably

Task 2

1

Archeologists, for example, help us to learn about the past. *They* look for evidence in artefacts like pots and jewellery. *These* reveal a lot of information about our ancestors. *This* is very useful, but *it* is still quite limited.

2

1 d 2 b 3 a 4 c

3

b Old buildings help <u>create a more relaxing environment</u> in cities than concrete office blocks.

c Studying history may <u>trigger an interest in other subject areas</u>.

d Built-up areas can be made more attractive by adding <u>monuments and statues</u>.

e Governments should <u>provide more money to preserve historical sites</u>.

f <u>Tradition</u> does not hold us back as some people believe.

g Schools and colleges need to emphasize <u>history and related subjects</u> …

h <u>The Internet and computers</u> can be used to preserve the past.

4

a it/this
b they
c This
d it, it
e it/this
f this
g this

5

Students' own answers.
Other important historical events could be the discovery of Australia, the discovery that the earth goes round the sun, or the first splitting of the atom.

6

Relevant points: b, d, e, g

7

Possible answers

… such as in Ancient Greece or during the Roman Empire.
As a result, they will be able to compare these societies with our own.
Therefore, they will become more aware of the kind of society that we live in.
Furthermore, they will come to appreciate the contribution that these societies made to the way we think today.

8

Students' own answers.

9

Possible answers

They could visit historical places such as castles or archaeological sites.
They could research their own family history.
They could do project work on historical periods or figures who interest them.

10

	Paragraph		
	1	2	3
Solutions	a	b	h
Examples	i	e	d
Effects	f	c	g

11

a	solution	b	effect
c	example	d	solution
e	example	f	example
g	effect	h	solution
i	effect		

12

Possible answers

One way is to encourage children to study history by using the Internet. For example, they could search for information about historical figures online. This could increase their motivation to do historical research.

The best way is probably to visit historical sites. For instance, children could visit a local archeological site. As a result, the historical places will come to seem more real.

Another method is to involve children in doing writing projects, such as producing a poster or an information booklet. The skills that they practise in these sorts of projects could then be applied in other subjects.

Unit 3

Task 1

1

Possible answers

a ring: gold, silver
   house: cement, stone, wood, glass
   bag: plastic
   shoe: leather
   car: steel, plastic, glass

b natural: gold, silver, stone, wood, leather
   manufactured: cement, glass, plastic, steel

2

1 is extracted
2 is heated
3 is cooled
4 reaches
5 cools
6 condenses

3

1 hold
2 rains
3 fill
4 becomes
5 occur
6 rises
7 begins
8 falls

4

a intransitive
b transitive
c both

Sentence a cannot be put into the passive.

5

Transitive: design, produce, send, manufacture, obtain, become
Intransitive: fall, rise, die
Both: begin, dry, grow, cool

6

Some variation is possible.

a After the motorcycle is designed, a prototype is made. It is tested and the motorcycle is manufactured. After this, it is exported and sold.

b First the wheat is planted, and later the crop is harvested. The wheat is transported to the mill where it is made into flour. The flour is bought by a baker. Later the bread is baked and sold.

7

1 b   2 c   3 a   4 h   5 d
6 e   7 f   8 g

8

a by conveyor belt
b oxygen
c raw syngas
d carbon dioxide, mercury and sulphur
e purified syngas
f It drives it.

g It powers it.
h the turbine
i They are sent to a heat recovery steam generator.

9

1 First of all
2 After that
3 where
4 From this
5 Following that
6 in turn
7 then
8 subsequently

10

a When the snow falls, it covers the ground with a protective layer.
b As soon as her cubs are born, the lioness licks them all over.
c Once the paper is collected, it is sent for recycling.
d Before volcanoes erupt, they send huge amounts of smoke into the air.
e When the plants perspire, the air becomes humid.
f The trees are cut down and the forest is gradually destroyed.

11

Possible answers

a As soon as the food is processed, it is packaged and then it is distributed.
b When the cycle is completed, it repeats itself all over again.
c After the rubbish is collected, it is sent to a centre for sorting and then it is recycled.
d Once a new model of the bicycle is developed, it is tested.
e When the TV is assembled, it is sent to the shops.
f As soon as the water is purified, it is bottled.
g The data about the weather is collected, and the information is then broadcast.
h Once the prototype has been tested, it is modified.

12

Students' own answers.

Task 2

1

Possible answers

a   Computers, automatic doors, mobile phones, and satellite navigation systems can all help. All of them can make life difficult as it can take some time to learn how to use them and they can go wrong.

b   Automatic doors and TV remote controls might make people lazier. Video games and MP3-players might also make people lazy in that people might come to prefer using these instead of taking up more active pastimes.

c   Students' own answers.

2

causes, solutions

3

a   practical skills for everyday life
b   over-reliance on machines
c   office functions, opening and locking doors, switching machines on and off
d   Workers cannot do basic practical tasks.
e   They have difficulty in processing basic information.

4

a   allow the TV to do their thinking for them at home
b   traditional practical skills

5

a   Sometimes computers make mistakes and prevent things happening, which wastes valuable time and can cost money.
b   TV programmes provide people with information about the world around them, which is often very useful.
c   Machines now give us more freedom, which means we have more time for leisure activities.

d   Technology saves us more and more time, which can be used to create more machines.
e   More and more household tasks are now carried out by robots, which will be even more common in the future.
f   Everything seems to be available at the touch of a button, which makes people expect instant responses from other people.

6

a   computers make mistakes and prevent things happening
b   information about the world
c   machines now give us more freedom
d   time
e   robots
f   everything seems to be available at the touch of a button

The *which*-clause expresses an effect in a, c, d, and f.

7

a   The situation, which has now become much more complex, is effectively out of control.
b   The problem, which the public blame the government for, is everyone's responsibility.
c   The cause of the problem, which is not immediately obvious to everyone, is a lack of basic training.
d   The solution, which in my opinion, is by far the best, is to have a day at work where people do not use computers or other machines.
e   Office technology, which requires only basic training to use, is the cause of much frustration at work.

8

Paragraph 2
Example: fixing a plug, mending a puncture on a bicycle, or even sewing a button on a shirt
Cause: parents no longer have enough time to spend at home with their children
Effect: young people are consequently deprived of valuable time to learn practical skills

Paragraph 3
Cause: international drive towards learning new technology
Result 1: young people leaving school literate in certain computer skills
Result 2: a generation almost deficient in basic practical skills
Reason: technical problem-solving has been squeezed out of the curriculum
Example: making things in carpentry

9

Paragra ph 1
Problem: First of all
Cause: A number of reasons have been put forward for this, but by far the most important

Paragraph 2
Example: like
Cause: because
Effect: consequently

Paragraph 3
Cause: also needs to carry a good part of the blame
Result 1: This has led to
Result 2: it has also created
Reason: because
Example: like

10

Result
so
therefore
consequently
as a result
and so
for this reason
as a consequence
hence
which leads to
which means that

Purpose
in order to
so as to
with the aim of
so that

11

Possible answers

a   Children are now learning how to do mental arithmetic again, which means that they will rely less on calculators.

b   Some cities charge motorists to take their cars into the centre in order to encourage people to use public transport.
c   Machines are manufactured to break down after a certain time, so that companies can sell more of them.

Unit 4

Task 1

1
Students' own answers

2
a   The pie charts describe the proportions of each group reading particular numbers of articles each week.
b   The numbers represent percentages of people.
c   It shows the number of articles read each week. There are three separate categories.
d   For all students, the most noticeable feature is that the majority read 1–5 articles.
    For PhD students, the most noticeable feature is that the majority read twelve or more articles per week.
    For junior lecturers, the most noticeable feature is that the majority read 6–11 articles per week.
e   In general, most students read between one and five articles a week.
    Most PhD students read more articles than other students and junior lecturers.
    A tiny minority of junior lecturers read only 1–5 articles per week.

3
a   how, and
b   For example,
c   respectively
d   whereas
e   Meanwhile,
f   but, which
g   that

4
Paragraph 1: a
Paragraph 2: b, c, d
Paragraph 3: e, f
Paragraph 4: g

5
General: a, e, g
Specific: b, c, d, f

6
General: b, d, e, f, g
Specific: a, c, h

7
a   Far fewer junior lecturers read over twelve articles a week compared with PhD students.
b   The average junior lecturer reads more journal articles than the average student.
c   The average PhD student reads more articles than the other students at the university.
d   Those students who are researching for a PhD have more time to read articles than junior lecturers.

8
26 per cent
about one in four
just over a quarter

33 per cent
one third
one in three

48 per cent
almost half
nearly half
just under one half
close to one half

75 per cent
three out of four
three quarters

9
very big: vast, overwhelming
very big (used before numbers): massive, hefty
very small: tiny
not very big (used before numbers): modest, mere

10
Possible answers
a   about one in four/just under a quarter
b   the overwhelming/vast majority of; 75 per cent
c   about one in three/just over one third; one in ten
d   Fifty per cent; a hefty 64 per cent/over six out of ten
e   The overwhelming/vast majority/About nine out of ten

11
a   The percentage who spent 8–14 hours in the library are similar: 35 per cent for all students and 32 per cent for postgraduate. The proportions are approximately the same, but for different categories of hours.
b   The percentages of students spending 1–7 hours and fifteen or more hours are very different in each case.
c   As students progress towards postgraduate level, the number of hours spent in the library increases.
d   The similarity between the different proportions for undergraduates and postgraduates, but for different categories.
e   Undergraduate students spend less time than other students in the library. Other students spend less time in the library than postgraduate students. Postgraduate students spend more time in the library than all other students.

12
a   pattern   e   trend
b   proportion   f   two-thirds
c   majority   g   quarter
d   minority

13
Students' own answers.

1

a They are connected by the topic of education.

b No, they stand alone. The statements are very sweeping and do not clearly support the first one.

c You could give reasons like: *because this would help poorer countries and poorer parts of rich countries develop.* Then you could give examples, like: *For example, schools in places like .... could be sponsored by richer countries.*

2

Both statements support the opinion.

3

Students' own answers.

4

Possible answers

a It is important that universities should make more links with businesses.

b There is no doubt that the present young generation knows more than their previous counterparts.

c One cannot deny that teaching thinking at school is essential, even at primary level.

d It is impossible to argue against the fact that more time needs to be devoted to learning music, either during or after school hours.

5

Possible answers

e Some people believe physical education is a necessary part of the learning process for all pupils.

f Some people feel that play is a major part of the learning process for children.

g Other people are of the opinion that it is important for children to try to learn another language early in their education.

h Yet other people put forward the view that being bored and learning to deal with boredom is a necessary part of the learning process for children.

6

e 1   d 2   c 3   b 4   5 g
6 a   7 f   8 h

7

a 3   b 2   c 1

8

Possible answers

a For example, they can learn languages like Japanese or Russian.

b A good example is the endless tests given to school children in some countries.

c Take for example trips to places of historical interest like The Great Wall of China or Istanbul.

d It can, for example, provide small classes and sometimes even better facilities.

e Famous sports stars like footballers could, for instance, conduct training on a regular basis.

9

Possible answers

a Some people are of the opinion that foreign language learning should be compulsory, because it helps intellectual development. It can, for instance, develop one's own language and improve communication.

b There is no doubt that students need to have good study skills on entering university, since most subjects require a lot of sophisticated skills like listening to lectures, note taking, etc.

c Yet others feel that university lecturers need some teacher training, as they are used to lecturing rather than teaching which is not suitable for small groups. Lecturers could, for instance, follow short courses or visit colleges or schools.

d It is important that boys and girls ought to be educated in separate schools. One reason for this is that they learn in different ways. For example, boys are known to prefer competitive activities.

e Some people think that teachers' salaries need to be as high as doctors' or lawyers' since they have such an important job to do. For instance, creating a future generation of doctors and lawyers requires good well-paid teachers in the present.

Unit 5

1

Suggested answers

a Dave thinks it was worse. There is now more for young people to do.
Sandra thinks it was better. It was quiet and peaceful. Now there is a bypass.
Tom agrees the town was prettier and more peaceful. However, he thinks there are more jobs and opportunities.

b Students' own answers.

c Dave: The ice rink, the leisure centre, and the skate park were opened by the council last year.
Sandra: A bypass and an industrial estate were built a few years ago.

d Students' own answers.

2

a The town changed considerably over the period.

b It was more residential.

c There were fewer trees in 2005.

d They were dramatic.

e The construction of the stadium and the removal of the houses.

f They were cut down and replaced by skyscrapers.

3

2 residential
3 experienced
4 noticeable
5 houses
6 factories
7 facilities
8 construction
9 corner
10 comparison

4

a The town centre was developed dramatically.
b The neighbourhood was completely transformed.
c The residential area was totally reconstructed.
d The old factories were totally redeveloped.
e The old houses were rebuilt.
f The entertainment district was completely modernized.

5

b The town centre developed dramatically.

6

a The map shows changes which *took place* between 1980 and 2005.
b Very few trees *remained*.
c Over the next 25 years, all these houses *were knocked down*.
d The single dwellings *made way for* skyscrapers.
e The trees *were cut down*.
f The area *experienced* dramatic changes.
g The woodland *made way for* a golf course.
h A marina *was also built*.

7

a was knocked down
b was cut down
c was redeveloped
d was converted
e underwent
f was pulled down/replaced
g was constructed
h took place
i was transformed

8

d cannot replace *Between 2000 and 2005*.

9

a By 2005, the row of old houses had been knocked down to make way for a road.
b By 2005, the forest had been cut down to build a railway.
c By 2005, the area had been redeveloped completely.
d By 2005, the factory had been converted into an art gallery.
e By 2005, the city centre had undergone a total transformation.
f By 2005, the row of old terraced houses in the city had been pulled down and replaced by a block of flats.
g By 2005, a sports complex had been constructed in the suburbs.
h By 2005, a number of spectacular changes had taken place.
i By 2005, the whole centre of the town had been transformed by new developments.

10

a They are beside the railway line.
b It is north-east of the lake.
c It is south-west of the stadium.
d It is south of the golf course.
e It is north of the skyscrapers.
f It is in the south-west of the town.
g It is south of the river.

11

a in   b by   c beside
d in   e from   f on
g beside h on   i off

Task 2

1

Students' own answers.

2

a You can agree or disagree completely. You can agree 50 per cent and disagree 50 per cent. You cannot be neutral. You have to express an opinion.
b Young employees should receive the same amount of money as older people if they do identical work.

3

a Opinion statement
b Contradiction
c Example
d Explanation
e Reason
f Reason
g Result

4

a Many people believe that
b However
c Take for example
d They deserve to receive the same salary …
e because
f Moreover,
g which

5

Students' own answers.

6

Delete the following:
1 Moreover
2 while
3 And
4 also
5 however
6 Subsequently

7

1 a contrast
2 b reason
3 a addition
4 c example
5 a result
6 c conclusion

8

Possible answers

a Many feel that young people have much more influence in the world than their counterparts in the past. Personally, I believe that this is not necessarily true, because most people in power belong to the older generation. For example, most politicians throughout the world are mainly middle-aged. Moreover, most wealth is concentrated among people in their forties upwards. So, young people may appear to exert influence, but it is limited.

b According to some people, older workers are just as equipped to deal with the modern world as young people. However, I think that younger people are much more prepared because they are much more computer-literate than older people. Moreover, they are well-acquainted with the latest 'gadgets'. For example, many young people are able to design their own web pages and adapt quickly to the latest tools. Thus, I feel they are better at coping with today's world.

c Some people are of the opinion that advertising should not be banned in TV programmes directed at young people. Nevertheless, I feel, adverts in these programmes should be stopped, as they encourage young people to buy products that neither they nor their parents can afford. Take the latest toys or HD television sets. Parents may be put under enormous pressure to buy these, thus ending up in debt. So I think some control must be exercised over TV commercials in programmes for young people.

9

1 a   2 c   4 b

10

Possible answer

Some people feel that weblogs are just a waste of time and another way to lure people on to the Internet. Personally, however, I feel that they are very useful for people of all ages, especially young people, for many reasons.

Unit 6

Task 1

1
Students' own answers.

2

Possible answers

Student exchanges, language learning, joint cultural events, and shared scientific, and technological know-how can be carried out by individuals. Trade agreements, transport links, and media images can be improved by governments. Tourism can be carried out by both individuals and governments. Climate and landscape, and lifestyle and culture are difficult to change.

3

a the overwhelming majority of people were in favour of

b with a smaller number naming lifestyle and food

c the most important languages, about equal numbers of people

4

a Sentence a relates to student exchanges, b relates to climate, and c relates to language learning.

b Sentence a is illustrated by pie chart 1, b is illustrated by pie chart 4, and c is illustrated by pie chart 3.

5

a pie chart 1
b pie chart 3
c pie chart 1
d pie chart 2
e pie chart 4

6

a The vast majority of holiday makers to China …

b It is clear that almost equal numbers of both sexes …

c Only a tiny minority of filmgoers …

d In conclusion, the trend is clearly upward, with just under half of companies …

e To sum up, nearly a third of all tourists …

7

Overall
It is clear that
To conclude
It is evident that
It would seem that
It is clear that
In conclusion
To sum up

8

a Backpacking is popular with the youngest group and guided tours relatively unpopular. This pattern is reversed for the oldest group.

b 31–40 year olds

c satisfied

9

2 enjoyed
3 belong
4 accounts for
5 comes
6 make up
7 include
8 is rated

10

It is clear …

11

a although, nevertheless

b *although* is a conjunction, *nevertheless* is an adverb. *Nevertheless* normally starts a sentence.

c but, however, despite

But is a conjunction, *however* is an adverb and normally starts a sentence. *Despite* can only be used before a noun or an *-ing* form.

12
a 3   b 1   c 5   d 2   e 4

13
a Although the vast majority of visitors to Britain come from Europe, they stay for fewer than ten days on average.
b Although forty-five per cent of people speak a foreign language, the vast majority are at a low level.
c Despite its/the good weather, southern France is visited by only two per cent of Asian tourists.
d The number of student exchanges rose, but/although the cost of them went up.
e Although the event was promoted to teenagers, they accounted for only 32 per cent of the audience.

Task 2

1
Students' own answers.

2
a the first sentence
b the second sentence (advantages and disadvantages)

3
(Some other entertainment devices may be possible.)

a Advantage: iPod, DVD player
b Advantage: Mobile phone.
c Disadvantage: iPod, handheld game.
d Advantage: iPod, handheld game.
e Advantage: iPod, mobile phone, handheld game, DVD player
f Disadvantage: iPod.
g Disadvantage: Mobile phone.
h Disadvantage: iPod, handheld game.

4
a benefits
b help
c difficult
d enable/help
e interfere
f ideal

5
Advantage: help, benefits, ideal, enable
Disadvantage: difficult, interfere, enable

6
a e
b for example, so, however, hence, nevertheless, because
c They allow people to relax; they allow people greater freedom; they are a nuisance for other travellers.

7
1 for example
2 even if
3 likewise
4 though
5 Although
6 and
7 Consequently

8
a disadvantage
b c, e, f, h
c Main advantage: *this allows people greater freedom and flexibility and takes away the boredom of journeys.*
Main disadvantage: *people are becoming more and more isolated in their own worlds. The art of communication is being lost.*

9
a drawbacks
b chance
c gain
d problems
e handicap
f opportunities
g benefit

10
Serious emphasizes disadvantage.

11
Advantage: advantageous, beneficial, useful, invaluable, helpful, convenient
Disadvantage: worthless, difficult

12
advantageous – disadvantageous
beneficial – detrimental
useful – useless
worthless – valuable/invaluable
invaluable – worthless
difficult – easy
helpful – unhelpful
convenient – inconvenient

13

Possible answers
a International arts festivals encourage interest in other people's cultures.
b Lending artworks to other countries improves their knowledge of other cultures.
c Films and concerts enhance the quality of people's lives.
d To enable children to value their heritage, we need to show them how strongly it still influences society today.
e Personal links can benefit travellers when they are out of their own country.
f Ignorance of other people's traditions can handicap business partnerships.
g To prevent countries from falling out with each other, we need to promote interest in particular cultures.

14
a 1 Although, 2 Despite
b 1 emphasizes the disadvantage, 2 emphasizes the advantage.

15
a Although
b However/Nevertheless
c Despite
d However/Nevertheless
e but

Unit 7

1

Students' own answers.

2

a   There was little change over the period, only a slight increase from each source.
b   The highest proportions were allocated by non-European countries (Japan and USA).
c   business
d   the EU average
e   The highest proportion was allocated by Japan, the lowest by Italy.

3

2   is shown   3   rose
4   came   5   contributed
6   overtook   7   was spent
8   contributed   9   was

4

slightly, approximately, consistently, closely, significantly, considerably

5

a   significantly
b   consistently
c   highly
d   slightly
e   marginally
f   considerably
g   Approximately
h   substantially

6

a 4   b 5   c 3   d 7   e 1
f 2   g 6

7

It is also noticeable that
It is interesting to note that

8

a   The number of scientists per head of population has declined significantly in recent years.
b   It is interesting that the sales failed to recover.
c   Numbers will probably continue to fall over the period.

d   Not surprisingly, there were skills shortages in the chemical industry.
e   It is evident that investment needs to be increased.
f   It is noticeable that the pattern for investment in the arts is the reverse.
g   It is more important that the cost of plasma screens is set to fall.
h   It is not surprising that analogue TV sales then fell.

9

Sentences b, c and d are possible.

10

a   The number of science graduates fell significantly.
b   Evidently, the number of technical staff in hospitals is falling.
c   The cost of training scientists is increasing noticeably year by year.
d   Interestingly, investment in capital equipment like specialist machinery is down on last year.
e   Not surprisingly, sales of new televisions soared before the World Cup.
f   The trend is now obviously upward.

11

Possible answers

a   Funding for R&D increased only marginally over the period.
    Business provided approximately half of the investment in 1998.
    The amount of funding increased very slowly over the period.
b   Japan allocated considerably more of its national income to R&D than Italy.
    Evidently, the four EU countries invested less than the USA or Japan.
    The proportion of national income given to R&D was noticeably higher in Germany and France than in Italy.
    The proportion allocated by the UK was only slightly above the EU average.
    Interestingly, the average

proportion among EU countries was below that for Japan and the USA.

12

a   students on all courses at an Australian university
b   seven
c   maths
d   physics, oriental languages
e   chemistry
f   Apparently not. For example, chemistry and physics are both science subjects but chemistry was seen as easy by 70 per cent of students and physics by only 25 per cent. Likewise, among language subjects, African languages were seen as easy by 60 per cent but oriental languages by only 20 per cent.

13

a   irrelevant
b   relevant
c   relevant
d   irrelevant because it contains an unnecessary opinion
e   relevant
f   irrelevant as it gives too much data, or rather unnecessary information about how the bar chart is drawn

14

Possible answer

The bar chart shows whether students at an Australian university rated different subjects as easy, moderately difficult, or difficult.
The subject which was most commonly rated as difficult was maths, by 70 per cent of students. Only 20 per cent saw it as easy. Physics was also largely judged to be a difficult or moderately difficult subject. Only 25 per cent of students viewed it as easy. By contrast, chemistry was regarded as easy by a massive 70 per cent of students.
As far as language subjects are concerned, languages in general were seen as easy by 40 percent of students. This percentage dropped to 20 percent for oriental languages. African languages, however, were viewed as easy by 60 per cent of students. Art was

judged to be an easy subject by only 30 per cent of students and, like physics, 50 per cent rated it as difficult.

In conclusion, there seems to be no clear correspondence between the type of subject and whether it was generally rated as easy or difficult.

Task 2

1

Students' own answers.

Background information:
Leonardo da Vinci was a famous Italian artist and inventor who painted the Mona Lisa.
Albert Einstein was a famous theoretical physicist who came up with the theory of relativity.
Sir Isaac Newton was an English scientist and mathematician who described the properties of gravity.
Nicolaus Copernicus was a Polish scientist who recognized that the Earth orbited the Sun.

2

a first sentence
b second sentence
c third sentence

3

1 c   2 b   3 a

4

Many people feel strongly; They argue; Supporters of arts groups feel

5

a 4   b 1   c 3   d 5   e 2
f 8   g 7   h 6

6

Possible answers

b Some people feel that the wealth of a nation is connected with scientific development. They claim that modern economies cannot advance without a strong scientific base.

c A commonly held belief is that science is now playing a more important role in our lives than in the past. People feel that it has an effect on everything we do from eating to travelling.

d It is argued by some people that the work of artists should be censored. They maintain that certain works of art that are produced are offensive and should be banned.

e Some people think that scientists should have some involvement with artists, and vice versa. They argue that bringing these two groups together would be better for society as a whole.

f Some people feel that science is dull and boring. They maintain that spending time alone in laboratories without much human contact is not very interesting.

g It is argued by some people that many scientific experiments are dangerous to society. They claim that there are many examples where serious mistakes have been made.

h Yet others believe that the work of scientists should not be tightly regulated by society. They argue that by limiting scientific work, we might stop certain beneficial developments.

7

Possible answers

b A good example here is Germany, which produces a large number of science graduates and has a thriving economy.

c For example, when we buy food from the supermarket the flavourings and additives have all been measured and tested scientifically.

d A case in point are certain works which depict religious figures.

e For example, more regular contact between the two would help scientists to appreciate the way in which scientific advances are perceived in society as a whole.

f Take the job of lab technician for instance. It involves dealing with tests and test results, and there is very little human contact involved.

g A good example is certain tests in which possible new medical drugs were tried out on humans only to find that they had unforeseen and very serious effects on the subjects' health.

h For instance, how could we continue to research cures for diseases such as cancer or AIDS if the non-scientific community were allowed to interfere with scientists' work?

8

a 2   b 5   c 4   d 1   e 3

9

would, could and *might* talk about possibility.
Sentence d asks the reader to imagine a situation and its consequence.

10

a Unless they are encouraged by parents and teachers, budding musicians will not develop.

b If science stops the ageing process in humans one day, will this benefit mankind?

c Unless there is an effort to keep traditional crafts alive, they will disappear.

d Providing innovation is encouraged, many new jobs will be created.

11

Possible answers

a Provided parents have an interest in music, they will encourage musical talent in their children.

b   If government support for arts projects is not available, they will be forced to seek funding elsewhere.

c   Unless entrance to museums and art galleries is free, many people will never experience them at all.

d   Providing young scientists are given the right opportunities, the work they do has the potential to be of enormous benefit to society.

Unit 8

Task 1

1

Possible answers

a   The photographs relate to our changing future relationship with the environment.

b–d   Students' own answers.

2

a   It shows predictions for the number of buildings that will be powered by solar and wind energy.

b   They relate to the number of houses.

c   0–600 million

3

a   will
b   predicted, will
c   prediction, will
d   predicted

4

a   projection, forecast, anticipation
b   projected, anticipated, forecast
c   prediction: expectation, estimation
    predicted: expected, estimated, set

5

a   is predicted, will provide
b   are expected
c   will come
d   is forecast
e   is not expected
f   is projected, will be
g   is set
h   is anticipated, will provide

6

Sentence *a* decribes something which will happen before a future time.
Sentence *b* describes something in progress at a time in the future.

7

a   will be using
b   will be living
c   will have been sold
d   will have become
e   will have been destroyed

8

a   the pie chart
b   It is projected to increase.
c   Ireland
d   Hungary
e   the pie chart
f   Yes, 64 per cent.

9

1   The charts show forecasts for the annual reforestation (*not deforestation*) rate in selected regions

2   They forecast that the reforestation rate in the four regions will grow until 2025 (*not 2035*)

3   It is projected that Ireland will have the highest rate in 2025 at 1.7 per cent (*not 1.5 per cent*)

4   It is anticipated that the figure will climb from 0.5 per cent in 2006 (*not 2015*)

5   with the worldwide average for both 2015 and 2025, 1.0 per cent and 1.3 per cent respectively (*not 1.3 and 1.0*)

6   ('concerned' 39 per cent, and 'very concerned' 25 per cent),

10

a   It *is* predicted that the use of solar energy will become more important.

b   We see from the chart that *the* largest amount of money was spent on the water conservation project.

c   The chart shows the different types of trees *which* are found in different regions.

d   From the pie chart, *it* can be seen that hydroelectric power constitutes seven per cent of the world energy demand.

e   It is clear that *the* majority of people are very concerned about climate change.

f   Recently, a number of campaigns have encouraged people *to* plant trees.

11

Generally, it *is* forecast that the reforestation rate
It is also worth noting that
From the pie chart, it can be seen that

12

a   It gives in thousands the estimated and actual numbers of houses built in the UK in 2002.

b   seven

c   below

d   Southern England (77,500), London (47,800) and in Central England (16,200). These figures far exceeded the estimates.

e   North of England. The estimate was 9,300 houses while the actual figure was 13,500.

f   Northern Ireland and Wales. In Wales, it was estimated that 2,900 houses would be built, but the real figure was 6,300. Likewise, in Northern Ireland the estimate was for 2,500 thousand houses, but the real number was 5,000.

g   Scotland.

h   Scotland. It was estimated that 3,200 houses would be built but in the event the figure was only 3,000.

13

Possible answer

The diagram gives figures for the actual and estimated numbers of houses built in the UK by region in 2002.

In most cases, the estimated number was below the number of houses which were actually built. The highest numbers of houses were constructed in Southern England (77,600), London (47,800), and in Central England (16,200), far exceeding the estimates (51,100, 24,800, and 8,100 respectively). Similarly in the North of England, there was a disparity of just over 4,000 between the two figures, 9,300 houses for the estimated figure against 13,500 for the actual figure. Northern Ireland and Wales followed the same trend, 2,500 houses as opposed to 5,000, and 2,900 compared to 6,300. Scotland was the region where the lowest number of houses were built. It was estimated that 3,200 houses would be constructed but in the event the figure was only 3,000.

In conclusion, it is clear that many more houses were built in the UK in 2002 than had been anticipated.

Task 2

1

Possible answers

a The most serious threats are water shortages, drought and other natural disasters, as well as other effects of global warming.

b–d Students' own answers.

2

2	factories	6	leisure
3	pollutants	7	pressure
4	fish	8	action
5	wildlife	9	incentives

3

animal – countable
information – uncountable
nature – uncountable
climate – uncountable
accommodation – uncountable
knowledge – uncountable
research – uncountable
weather – uncountable
tree – countable
idea – countable
situation – countable
fact – countable

4

problem – countable
factories – countable
pollutants – countable
fish – uncountable
wildlife – uncountable
leisure – uncountable

pressure – uncountable
action – uncountable
incentives – countable

5

a no article, no article
b no article
c the
d a, no article
e no article
f the
g The, no article
h The

6

a Wave power technology is the best answer to the problem of pollution. However, the introduction of such technology also creates *a* problem.

b Governments worldwide should tax ~~the~~ cars more. A measure like this would make people think more about nature.

c In *the* near future, houses will be more energy-efficient than they are now.

d *The* food industry could pay for recycled bottles as was done in the past. The bottles would then not be thrown away.

e Insects like ~~the~~ bees, for example, play a vital role in most ecosystems. The bee pollinates plants and flowers.

f ~~The~~ Facilities like dams and forests are also used for leisure.

7

a 1   b 2   c 2   d 1   e 2
f 1   g 2

8

Question 1
Statement of most important measure: d
Another possible measure and why it is less effective: f
Restatement of most important measure and its consequences: a

Question 2
Statement of opinion: b
Reference to the opposite view: e
Reason against the opposite view: g
Restatement of opinion: c

9

In conclusion: to sum up, to conclude
I do not agree: I do not accept, I disagree with the idea that
All in all: in general, all things considered
I feel that: I believe, I would argue that
certainly: of course, no doubt

10

a There is no reason why local eco-friendly businesses cannot be successful.

b There is no reason why people could not take more holidays at home instead of always flying abroad.

c There is no reason why people could not travel by fast train instead of taking short flights.

d There is no reason why governments should not give special financial support to eco-friendly business people.

Unit 9

Task 1

1

Students' own answers.

2

a The graph gives information about the average use of beds in three typical hospitals around the world before and after day-surgery is introduced.

b While the trend was upward for the French hospital, the average bed occupancy dropped noticeably after the introduction of day-surgery.

c The trend for the Ukrainian hospital was similar to that of the French hospital, but the fall in bed use after 2003 was not as marked.

d You can make a connection between the coincidental fall in the budget for inpatient care and the fall in bed occupancy.

e You can use *trend* to summarize information.
You can use *upward* to show the direction of the trend.
You can use the phrase *similar pattern* to compare similarities.
You can use *reach a peak* to describe a high point.
You can use *except that* to introduce detail which is different from the general trend/pattern.
You can use *saw a continuous rise* as an alternative to *rose*.
You can use *change* to describe a difference that occurs.
You can use *coincide* to show when things happen at the same time, whether they are related or not.

3

2 impact
3 trend
4 occupancy
5 peak
6 falling
7 marked
8 experienced
9 rise
10 significantly
11 clear
12 reduction

4

1 details – information
2 impact – effect
3 trend – tendency
4 occupancy – use
5 peak – high point
6 falling – dropping
7 marked – sharp
8 experienced – saw
9 rise – increase
10 significantly – considerably
11 clear – evident
12 reduction – cut/decrease

5

Incorrect answers to be deleted:
a says
b had an affect on
c reached a height
d design
e alternatively
f towards

g contrast with
h can be viewed in

6

a 1 b 3 c 5 d 7 e 2
f 6 g 4 h 8

7

a before
b receive
c studying
d useful
e personally
f sufficient
g definitely
h different
i choice
j referred

8

Spelling rules
i before *e*, except after *c*: *receive*, but not after *ch*: *achieve*.
Words ending in a vowel then *y*: *y* does not change, eg *studying*.
Noun + *full*: remove the second *l* = *useful*.
Adverbs from adjectives ending in -*al*: add -*ly* and remove nothing, eg *personally*.
Adeverbs from adjectives ending in -*e* : add -*ly* and keep the *e*, eg *definitely*.
Verbs ending with *y* + -*ing*: no change, eg *studying*.
Words of more than one syllable: the consonant doubles if the final syllable is stressed: *referred*.

9

a gradually
b which
c occurred
d peak
e figures, approximately
f fluctuated
g exceeded
h survey

10

average
accidents
dramatically
improvement
steadily
regards
motorcycle
occurring

1

Student's own answers.

2

1 strangely
2 well
3 surprisingly
4 widely
5 accurately
6 often
7 seriously
8 well
9 frequently
10 Clearly

3

The paragraph follows sentence pattern a.

Organizing words
Situation: The *idea*
Example: Take the *example* of
Effects: The *effects*
Conclusion: the *conclusion* is

4

a information
b idea
c scheme
d measure
e issue
f solution
g knowledge
h opinion
i problem

5

Possible answers
a This issue needs to be considered when planning the health care budget for any country.
b This idea could have benefits both for people's health and the education of doctors and nurses.
c This prediction may seem surprising, but I believe costs will be reduced as technology becomes more widely available.
d Initially, this may be a problem, but the changes will result in a more efficient health service.
e The situation, however, is one that can be prepared for by setting money aside for the future.

f   Measures like this could lead to a significant improvement in the nation's health.

g   Not surprisingly, it is a trend which is not looked on favourably by some western doctors.

h   This is a matter that needs to be considered when planning for future spending.

6

Possible answers

a   music and health
Effect: helps people relax, takes up attention.
Measure: music therapy, used sometimes to treat patients with communication problems.

b   alternative therapies and health
Example: homeopathy, herbalism.
Information: contested by different people.
Opinions: health practitioners versus people who have experienced these therapies.
Effects: may be due to influence on the mind as well as body.

c   exercise and health
Effects: strengthens muscles, helps coordination, helps people to relax.
Problem: high cost of gyms/ health centres.
Scheme: companies offer gym membership as part of package to staff.

7

Students' own answers.

8

a is   b has   c are   d is
e has   f are   g is   h have

9

a   This information is published all around us, even on cigarette packets.

b   Unfortunately, this advice is not often followed.

c   Instead, this work is carried out by health care assistants.

d   Enormous progress has been made in understanding how disease spreads, …

e   However, this equipment can be dangerous if it is not used properly.

f   However, there is certainly some evidence that it is more than just a placebo.

g   Some research has been carried out which shows that elderly people live longer if they live with a partner.

Unit 10

Task 1

1

Students' own answers.

2

a   Both charts refer to the main reasons for choosing a career according to age group.

b   They refer to the reasons under consideration.

c   They show the different ways in which the two age groups were influenced by the various factors.

d   The most noticeable features are the importance of money and the position of friends.

e   The most noticeable features are the importance of money and parents, the reverse of the younger age group.

3

1   the main reasons for choosing a career
2   were influenced by the various factors
3   were the reverse for the 40–50 age group
4   As regards teachers and role models
5   nine and fifteen per cent respectively for the younger group
6   The only similarity between the two age groups
7   than any other factors

4

a   The sales of *specialist* tours have fallen recently.

d   It is clear that the number of flats *occupied* by single people in major cities in the West is putting pressure on housing.

e   From the graphs, it can be concluded that young people *are* much more mobile than previous generations.

f   The pursuit of a professional career among both men and woman has led to a *noticeable* reduction in the birth rate.

g   There are *several* similarities in the presentation of the data.

h   Overall, the chart shows that the media are responsible for turning *people* into celebrities.

5

a   an explanation
b   *with* is normally followed by a noun then a verb with *-ing*.

6

a   Sales were upward for most of the year, with the profit reaching a peak in December.

b   The main reason for career choice was ambition, with 50 per cent choosing it.

c   It is expected that the price of one bedroom flats will rise, with accommodation for individuals being in short supply.

d   The pattern was different, with passenger numbers dropping in summer and rising in winter.

e   The trend was clearly upward, with manufacturing costs decreasing at the same time.

f   Consumption of energy rose, with the highest point being in January.

7

a   True   b   False   c   False
d   False   e   True   f   False
g   False   h   True

1

Question 1: b, a, c
Question 2: b, d, a, c
Question 3: c, d, b, a

2

Question 1: a
Question 2: c
Question 3: b

3

Possible answers

Money does not make happiness. To what extent do you agree or disagree?
It is impossible to deny that money helps people to achieve happiness because it is impossible to do anything in life without it. For example, if you want to see a film or a play at the theatre, you need money for the ticket and for transport. Also, if you want to have a relaxing time at home you still need money, even to buy a TV or a computer. (structure b)
It is better to reform criminals instead of just punishing them. What measures could be taken to attempt to integrate law-breakers back into society?
Personally, I think that criminals of all levels should be given a chance to be a part of society rather than just being put into prison. If this is done, then the offender will have a better chance of not reoffending. Society will also not have to pay for the cost of keeping criminals in prisons, which are very expensive places to run. Of course, then society as a whole will benefit. (structure c)

4

Text 1
1 b   2 a   3 a

Text 2
4 a   5 b   6 b

Text 3
7 a   8 b

5

Students' own answers.

6

If you want to achieve a good score band, you need to be able to tick *Always* for all of the items in the list.

7

Possible answers

a for example, for instance, a case in point is, like
b as, one reason for this is, since
c as a result, therefore, so, this means that, this leads to
d moreover, furthermore, in addition, and, also
e if, unless, provided
f but, however, while, whereas, despite
g although, despite
h and so, and therefore, to sum up, all in all, in general

8

Suggested answers

a Problem and solution
b Measures and results
c Cause and effect
d Reason and example
e Example and specific example
f Effect and example
g Additional information and example
h Condition/Hypothesis and result
i Concession and contrast

9

Possible answers

a Money is not as important as friends, because it cannot provide emotional support.
b For many people, keeping fit and healthy is the main factor which is necessary for a good quality of life. However, developing a healthy mind is just as important.
c If one is content with life, then there is no longer any need to pursue unrealistic ambitions.
d What is involved in achieving a good quality of life depends on many factors rather than just one. For example, money is important to gain a certain financial security, but it is not enough on its own.
e Happiness and contentment are more important than the pursuit of freedom. The latter aim is an illusion as nobody is ever completely free.
f Many people living in poor housing conditions are still happy. So the idea that you have to have a high standard of living to be happy is false.

10

Possible answer

And yet other people believe that the family plays an important role in maintaining a good quality of life. You just have to look at societies where there are extended families to see how much more content people are because they are surrounded by relatives who love them and can look after them if they fall ill or have problems. This support is not just financial but also emotional.